NEW ENGLAND REMEMBERS

The Boston Strangler

Alan Rogers

Robert J. Allison, Series Editor

Commonwealth Editions
Beverly, Massachusetts

ISBN-13: 978-1-889833-52-1
ISBN-10: 1-889833-52-5

Library of Congress Cataloging-in-Publication Data

Rogers, Alan, 1936–
　　The Boston Strangler / Alan Rogers.
　　　p. cm. — (New England Remembers)
　　ISBN 1-889833-52-5 (alk. paper)
　　1. De Salvo, Albert Henry, 1931– 2. Murder—Massachusetts—Boston—
Case studies. 3. Murder—Investigation—Massachusetts—Boston—Case Studies.
I. Title. II. Series.
　　HV6534.B6.R64 2006
　　364.152'30974461—dc22
　　　　　　　　　　　　　　　　　　　　2006006029

Cover and interior design by Laura McFadden Design, Inc.
laura.mcfadden@rcn.com

Printed in the United States of America.

Commonwealth Editions
266 Cabot Street, Beverly, Massachusetts 01915
www.commonwealtheditions.com

Front cover photo: Albert DeSalvo emerging from the Lynn, Massachusetts, police station following his escape from Bridgewater State Hospital on February 24, 1967. Courtesy of Bettman/Corbis.

Back cover photo: Albert DeSalvo arriving at the Cambridge District Court on January 12, 1967. Courtesy of the Boston Globe.

The New England Remembers series
Robert J. Allison, Series Editor
The Hurricane of 1938
The Big Dig
The Cocoanut Grove Fire
Sacco and Vanzetti
Lizzie Borden

The "New England Remembers" logo features a photo of the Thomas Pickton House, Beverly, Massachusetts, used courtesy of the Beverly Historical Society.

CONTENTS

FOREWORD

BETWEEN JUNE 1962 AND JANUARY 1964, a mysterious killer terrorized women living alone in the Boston area. Over these months, thirteen women were found murdered inside their locked apartments.

Historian Alan Rogers tells the stories of these murders and of the investigation that followed. The police relied upon the usual investigative techniques, focusing their attention on men previously convicted of sexual assault, mental patients, and gay men. The special Strangler Bureau also used novel tools, including a computer, a lie detector machine, hypnosis, the advice of several psychiatrists, and the services of on an eccentric Dutch psychic. Despite these extraordinary efforts, the grisly murders continued, and the police had no suspect in custody and no solid leads to the killer. Eleven months after the final strangling, Albert DeSalvo, a prisoner at the Center for the Treatment of Sexually Dangerous Persons at Bridgewater, awaiting trial for several dozen sexual assaults, confessed to murdering thirteen women.

Although DeSalvo confessed to being the Boston Strangler, he was never brought to trial for those murders. Rather, he was tried and convicted for a string of nonlethal sexual assaults and sentenced to life in prison. He first was sent to the State Prison for the Criminally Insane in Bridgewater and then, after his escape, sent to Walpole State Prison. DeSalvo was stabbed to death in his locked cell at Walpole in 1973. His murder, like those of the Strangler's victims, was never officially solved.

Alan Rogers weaves together the many strands of this troubling and tragic story. Boston's transition from being a staid city dominated by Yankee financial institutions and Irish-American political power to a self-proclaimed progressive "New Boston" is the background for this grisly story of sexual deviance and murder. Though there have been other serial killers since, and though police work and forensic science have far advanced in the short time since 1962, New England remembers the Boston Strangler, as well as his victims.

Robert J. Allison, Series Editor
Boston, Massachusetts

INTRODUCTION

BETWEEN JUNE 14, 1962, AND JANUARY 4, 1964, thirteen Boston women were murdered inside their locked apartments. With one exception, each victim was partially clothed, propped in a sexually suggestive pose with a nylon stocking or undergarment tied in a floppy bow around her neck. Every Boston woman feared she could be the next victim of the "Boston Strangler." Despite efforts by the Boston police, a special Strangler Bureau created by the Massachusetts Attorney General, the Federal Bureau of Investigation, and a Hollywood psychic—as well as thousands of tips phoned in by citizens—the murderer was not arrested or officially identified. The string of murders ended as suddenly as they had begun.

Ten months after the last murder, on November 5, 1964, Cambridge police arrested Albert DeSalvo for sexual assault. DeSalvo, 33, was a fast-talking criminal known locally as the "Measuring Man" because he pretended to be a talent scout for female models in order to fondle them. When the police broadcast his picture, police in Connecticut identified him as the "Green Man," wanted for dozens of sexual assaults in that state. Might DeSalvo have been the Boston Strangler?

DeSalvo was committed to Bridgewater State Hospital for psychiatric observation. In that fetid, brutal facility he befriended convicted murderer George Nassar. DeSalvo told Nassar details of the stranglings and Nassar called his attorney, F. Lee Bailey. On March 4 the brilliant young attorney agreed to represent DeSalvo, and two days later Bailey heard DeSalvo's confession to the murders. DeSalvo confessed not only to murdering the eleven women police originally had attributed to the strangler, but also to killing two more, sixty-nine-year-old Mary Brown and eighty-five-year-old Mary Mullen. Because DeSalvo was a mental patient, his confession couldn't be used against him in court, and he pleaded not guilty by reason of insanity to the sexual assault charges. Was DeSalvo legally insane, or was he a street-smart murderer trying to escape the full impact of the law?

The killings and their aftermath raised important questions about women's vulnerability and powerlessness in the emerging New Boston, about the alleged link between homosexuality and violence, and about the death penalty. These questions shaped and continue to define the memory of those events that gripped Boston in the early 1960s. We begin with the murders.

THE
BOSTON STRANGLER'S VICTIMS

Anna Slesers, age 55, June 14, 1962, Boston

Mary Mullen, age 85, June 28, 1962, Brighton
*Mullen's death was attributed to natural causes, but
DeSalvo later confessed he had his arm around her neck
when she collapsed, apparently from a heart attack.*

Helen Blake, age 65, June 30, 1962, Lynn

Nina Nichols, age 68, June 30, 1962, Brighton

Ida Irga, age 75, August 19, 1962, Boston

Jane Sullivan, age 76, August 20, 1962, Dorchester

Sophie Clark, age 20, December 5, 1962, Boston

Patricia Bissette, age 23, December 30, 1962, Boston

Mary Brown, age 69, March 9, 1963, Lawrence

Beverly Samans, age 23, May 6, 1963, Cambridge

Evelyn Corbin, age 58, September 8, 1963, Salem

Joann Graff, age 23, November 23, 1963, Lawrence

Mary Sullivan, age 19, January 4, 1964, Boston

CHAPTER ONE

Five Older Women

oston was a city of nearly seven hundred thousand in
the summer of 1962. It was also in the throes of urban
renewal: work on the fifty-two-story glass and steel
Prudential Center was underway, and plans were being
developed to renovate the old Quincy Market district. Before the
"New Boston" fully emerged in the late 1960s, the town known as the
"Cradle of Liberty" and the "Hub of the Universe" was characterized
by economic decline and sharp political infighting between Yankee
and Irish politicians.

Like urban centers throughout the United States, Boston had seen
an increase in crime and murder in the late 1950s. Over the course of
the 1960s, the number of murder victims in Boston would increase
from fifty each year to more than one hundred. Most of the murders
were domestic or drunken quarrels that turned violent or robberies that
went wrong. Police used simple investigative techniques to solve these
crimes: questioning eyewitnesses, scouring the crime scene for physical
evidence, dusting for fingerprints. Police usually made quick arrests and
obtained confessions, and the cases typically were closed in a matter of
months.

Murder victims usually were "nobodies" who lived in Boston's
seedy neighborhoods; their violent deaths were reported briefly, if at all,

1

on the daily newspapers' inside pages. Bostonians did not feel threatened. They were confident that the police were doing their job. But this confidence was shaken just a few months before the first murders attributed to the Strangler.

Early in 1962 a CBS television documentary titled "Biography of a Bookie Joint" exposed widespread corruption within the Boston Police Department. Police officers were shown entering and leaving illegal off-track betting establishments. The television exposé, and his alleged profligate spending habits, spelled the end for Police Commissioner Leo J. Sullivan. The new commissioner, Edmund McNamara, a graduate of Holy Cross and a former FBI agent, promised to eliminate graft and corruption and to streamline and update the force to fight crime better. Just a few weeks after he took office, however, McNamara had to put aside his reform agenda to try to solve a string of murders.

♟   ♟   ♟

FIFTY-FIVE-YEAR-OLD ANNA SLESERS was a Latvian immigrant who had come to the United States in 1950. Until recently she had lived with her son, Juris, an engineer at Lincoln Laboratories, but now she lived in a small third-floor apartment on Gainsborough Street, in the Back Bay, chosen so she could walk to Symphony Hall.

On the evening of June 14, 1962, Juris came to drive his mother to Roxbury for a special church service honoring Latvian soldiers killed in World War II. Shortly before seven o'clock, he knocked on her apartment door. There was no answer. He went back to the street, pacing up and down the sidewalk in front of the building. A few minutes passed. He bounded up the stairs and knocked more loudly on the door. Still no answer. He tried the door but found it locked. Going downstairs again, he noticed that his mother had not picked up her mail that day. Worried that she might be ill, he raced back upstairs. After pounding on the door, he took a couple of steps back, lowered his shoulder, and rammed into the door. On the second try, the door gave way. He stepped into the dimly lit apartment.

Juris slowly groped his way around the apartment. Looking into the bedroom, he noticed that the dresser drawers were open. He glanced into the kitchen and saw his mother's purse and glasses on a table. Then, as he turned toward the bathroom, he saw his mother's body sprawled on the floor in the hallway between the kitchen and the bathroom. Her housecoat was bunched up around her neck and shoulders, exposing her naked body. The cord from her housecoat was tied tightly around her neck in a bow.

Juris called the police, who arrived within minutes, followed by two veteran homicide detectives, Edward Sherry and John Donovan. The detectives determined that Anna Slesers had suffered a head injury before being strangled and that she had been sexually molested. The police interviewed dozens of Slesers's neighbors as well as painters and workmen who had been in and around the building. No one had seen a stranger enter or leave the building. One theory was that a painter's scaffold, which hung outside the unlocked third-floor window, might have allowed a robber to enter the apartment—and that when Slesers unexpectedly confronted the intruder he panicked and murdered her. *The Boston Globe* ran a brief story.

Although they were busy investigating other murders, Sherry and Donovan followed up their initial investigation by interviewing the people at a decorating firm downtown where Slesers worked. Her coworkers described her as conscientious and friendly, but they were unable to tell the police anything about her social life or her friends. After two weeks of investigative work, the detectives had no clues and no suspect.

What they soon had, however, was a second victim. At about five o'clock on Saturday, June 30, sixty-eight-year-old Nina Nichols was in her fashionable Commonwealth Avenue apartment, talking on the phone with her sister. "Excuse me, Marguerite," she said, "there's my buzzer. I'll call you right back." But she did not call back. And although she was due at her sister's Wellesley home at seven for dinner, by seven-thirty she still had not arrived. Marguerite tried calling and got no answer. At that point, Marguerite's husband, attorney Chester C. Steadman, president of the Boston Bar Association, called Thomas Bruce, the Commonwealth Avenue building's superintendent, and asked him to look out his window to see if Nichols's car was outside. Bruce saw that it was. Steadman asked him to check Nichols's apartment. Bruce knocked loudly on the door of the fourth-floor apartment, and when she didn't answer, he used his passkey to enter.

The apartment was a mess. Drawers had been pulled open, and clothing and other items were strewn over the floor. Then, as Bruce stood frozen at the threshold, he saw Nina Nichols's partially clothed body lying on the bedroom floor, her feet pointing straight at him. She was wearing a pink housecoat, which was torn and bunched up around her waist. A stocking had been tied so tightly around her neck that it had cut grooves into her flesh. The ends of the stocking had been turned up like a bow. Bruce ran to his telephone to call the police.

Detective Sherry surveyed the scene with a trained eye. Nichols had been criminally molested, probably after she was unconscious or dead. There was no sign of forcible entry. Sherry noted that although the apartment had been "tossed," robbery did not appear to be the motive. Nichols's watch was still on her wrist, a $300 camera lay in plain sight, and $5 was in her purse. It didn't seem possible that Nichols would have opened her door to a stranger. Although her murder was similar to the murder of Anna Slesers, and occurred only sixteen days afterward and a few blocks away, the police did not immediately see a connection.

Widowed for nearly twenty years, Nichols had worked part-time as a physiotherapist at Massachusetts General Hospital. She also volunteered at an old people's home. She had lots of women friends she visited on a regular basis—she had just returned from three days with a friend in Duxbury—and she loved photography and music. Neighbors said Nichols's brother-in-law was the only man they ever saw entering her apartment. Once again the police were without a clue or a suspect.

On Monday, July 2, at about 7 P.M., two elderly women in Lynn, north of Boston, became worried about their sixty-five-year-old friend Helen Blake. They had not seen Helen since Saturday, so they asked her building superintendent for a key to Blake's second-floor apartment. They shrieked when they opened the door. The apartment had been ransacked. In the living room a desk drawer lay on the floor, its contents scattered nearby. In the bedroom, drawers had been flung open—and Blake's body was lying facedown on the bed. Her pajama bottoms lay in a heap on the floor and a silk stocking and a bra were tied around her neck. The medical examiner determined that Blake had been murdered sometime Saturday morning, the same day of the week as

Boston police rounded up hundreds of suspects for questioning after the rash of stranglings began in June 1962. (Boston Globe)

Nichols. There was no sign of forced entry, and Blake's door had a chain and a bolt, leading District Attorney John Burke to suggest that Blake's killer "was apparently someone she knew."

Blake's neighbors thought that unlikely. They had never seen Blake with a man. She lived a quiet, modest life, eking out a living by accepting the occasional private nursing job. She entertained her friends by telling their fortunes with cards and by playing the piano. She loved music and whenever she could afford it, she attended concerts in Lynn and Boston.

Detective John Donovan, chief of Boston Homicide, came to Lynn to see first-hand the similarities between Blake's murder and those of Slesers and Nichols. Donovan did not comment, but the *Boston Globe's* front page called it "Another Silk Stocking Murder." The article quoted an unnamed police source as stating that the same man could have killed all three women. When Commissioner McNamara was told of Blake's murder, he blurted out: "Oh, God, we've got a madman loose!"

On the Fourth of July the *Boston Globe* announced that the police had launched a "feverish search for clues" to the killer's identity, a " 'round-the-clock hunt for a madman believed responsible for the strangling of three women." McNamara assigned all detectives to the homicide division. He urged women living alone to keep their doors locked and to not admit anyone without positive identification. To assist police, and to assuage women's fears, an emergency telephone number was published in all the city's newspapers and was broadcast by a dozen radio stations. Known sex offenders were rounded up and questioned, as were men between the ages of eighteen and forty who had recently spent time in mental institutions. Experts in the behavior of sexual predators were brought in to tutor Boston homicide detectives.

When seventy-five-year-old Ida Irga was found murdered in her West End apartment, Loretta McLaughlin, a reporter for the *Boston Record American*, wrote what everyone feared: all women were potential victims merely because they were women. The police were shocked by what they saw at Irga's fifth-floor apartment just before eight o'clock on the evening of August 21. They did not reveal to the public the most appalling details, only that the elderly woman's nude body was found lying face-up on the floor of a hallway connecting the kitchen and the living room. Like the other victims, the medical examiner noted that Irga had been strangled using the arm choke; from behind someone had caught her neck in the crook of his arm and exerted pressure. A pillowslip was tied around her neck. She had been dead for about two days. The *Globe* reported that Irga had been criminally assaulted. Again, there was no sign of a forcible entry.

Police withheld the brutal details of Irga's murder not only because they were so shocking but also because investigators wanted facts known only to the police and the killer. But police reports carried the ugly details. Irga's body had been placed so that it could be seen as soon as someone opened the apartment door. Her nightdress had been torn up the front to expose her entire body, and a pillow had been placed under her buttocks. Her legs were spread wide apart, her feet locked between the rungs of two chairs in a parody of the position for a gynecological examination The murderer had stripped his victim of life and dignity and, it seemed, had tried to shock and to mock the police.

Irga's neighbors described her as a "meticulous person who kept to herself." Her friends told police that she rarely went far from her home and never ventured out at night except to walk to a summer concert on the Esplanade. Acting on an anonymous tip, Detective Donovan and Sergeant Leo Gannon flew to Rye, New York, three days after Irga's death to question a man who had left town shortly after the murder. They questioned the man—identified by the press only as "a member of a prominent family"—for hours before concluding that he had nothing to do with Irga's murder. While Donovan and Gannon were in New York, Detective Sherry questioned and released a dozen known sex offenders in Boston. Commissioner McNamara acknowledged, "It leaves us right back where we started." He quickly added a warning to older women living alone to keep their doors securely locked. Several Boston locksmiths reported an increased demand for locks and for deadbolts.

A week after Irga's murder, Detectives Sherry and Donovan tried to answer the question of whether there was one Strangler or more than one preying on women living alone. The victims were from different economic backgrounds and different social classes, and they lived in different parts of the city. Still, Sherry clung to the assumption that something linked the four women together and that when he found

The Animal Rescue League reported in September 1962 that requests for dogs by older Boston women frightened by the string of stranglings were "unbelievable." (Boston Globe)

what that something was, he would find the killer or killers. We have to assume, he said, that one man could have committed the four murders (Slesers, Nichols, Irga, and Blake), but "we have not been able to find a single common denominator among the victims." While the police worked to discover how the victims were linked, another murder had occurred: Jane Sullivan, 67, of Dorchester had been strangled the same day as Ida Irga. She wasn't missed until August 30, when her nephew found her in her first-floor apartment on Columbia Road. There was no sign of a struggle, nor was there evidence of forcible entry into the apartment. No unidentified fingerprints were found. Described as "a beautiful grey-haired woman who looked much younger than her years," Sullivan recently had moved into the apartment because the bus she took home from her late-night job at Longwood Hospital stopped right outside her door.

The police again withheld crucial, gruesome details from the press, but their report noted that Sullivan had been strangled to death with two of her own nylon stockings tied together. The knot used—a combination of a granny knot, a square knot, and a double half hitch—was the same as the ligatures around the other victim's necks. From the room where Sullivan was murdered, her murderer then carried her body to the bathroom and placed it facedown in a partially filled bathtub so that her buttocks were exposed. The police assumed she had been sexually assaulted, but the body was so badly decomposed that they had to wait for further test results to be certain.

Now with five victims, Boston police believed they had the common thread for which they had been looking. All the Strangler's victims had some connection with hospitals or medical clinics. For that reason, police began checking all present and former employees of greater Boston hospitals and searching for an ex-mental patient known to have a history of choking women. Police theorized that such a man could have worked in Boston hospitals and come into contact with women he later victimized. Police also theorized that the Strangler dressed as a woman in order to gain access to his victim's apartments.

Three days after Irga's body was found, the *Boston Herald* tried to calm a badly frightened city by publishing an editorial calling for reason. "Hysteria Solves Nothing," the paper proclaimed. "It may be fairly said the police are looking for a needle in a haystack, but it may be said with equal validity that a given person's chances of becoming a victim of the killer or killers are almost nil." Any reassuring effect caused by the newspaper's appeal likely was erased six days later, when the body of the fifth victim, Jane Sullivan, was discovered.

CHAPTER TWO

Six Young Women

A little more than two weeks after the murders of Ida Irga and Jane Sullivan, Dr. Richard Ford, Suffolk County medical examiner and chair of the Department of Legal Medicine at Harvard University, called a summit meeting of New England's top medical examiners, psychiatrists, and law enforcement officials to exchange ideas about the stranglings. Although Ford declared the three-hour meeting beneficial, he admitted that the participants had not identified a common denominator among the murders, nor had they determined if there was one killer or several, nor had they concluded if the killings were incidental to the sexual assaults or the assaults incidental to the killings. Against this background, not surprisingly, Commissioner McNamara said there were "no prime suspects" and he did not know if, or when, the killer would strike again. He issued his standard warning: women living alone should keep their doors locked and not admit any stranger.

Dr. Phillip Solomon, chief of psychiatry at Boston City Hospital, was certain that there was one killer and that the killer would strike again. He agreed to provide a hypothetical psychological sketch of the Strangler for the press. The killer, Solomon wrote, probably appears to be a hard-working, law-abiding citizen, and he may even be polite and well mannered. He probably has above-average intelligence but works at a menial, uninteresting job, perhaps at a hospital where he can catch a glimpse of women clad only in examination gowns. Solomon also believed the murderer was about age forty and physically small—which gave him a crippling inferiority complex. Most important, the man responsible for these brutal crimes, according to Solomon, was "a psychotic sex pervert suffering from a most malignant form of schizophrenia." A severe, unloving mother may have triggered this rare and dangerous perversion. For this reason, the Strangler attacked older women because of deep-seated fear of a younger woman's sexual attraction. Finally, Solomon warned: "He will kill again unless the police get to him first."

Part of Solomon's theory—that the Strangler sought out only older women—was disproved shortly, when the next victim turned out to be twenty years old. Five other young women would follow.

On December 5, 1962, just days after Commissioner McNamara announced that one hundred more detectives had been assigned to investigate the strangling murders, twenty-year-old Sophie Clark, an African-American student and medical technician, was found lying dead faceup on the living room rug of her fourth-floor Back Bay apartment. She had been gagged and strangled with three of her own nylon stockings, and like the Strangler's other victims, Clark was either dead or unconscious before she had been sexually assaulted. Her bathrobe was open and she still wore her black loafers. There was evidence of a struggle. Her bra had been violently torn from her body, and her glasses lay broken on the floor near her body. The bureau drawers had been searched, and the murderer had rifled through Clark's record collection in the living room.

When a friend came to find out why Clark had not answered the phone that afternoon, she had to unlock the double lock on the door— a lock that Clark herself had insisted be installed in the wake of the murders. Neighbors said that Clark and her roommates were "very careful" about who they let into the apartment, and yet Clark, like the Strangler's other victims, had opened the door to the murderer.

In addition to the obvious differences—Clark was young and African-American and she did not live alone—this time the police had information about two likely suspects and perhaps a third. Earlier on the afternoon of the murder, a female neighbor of Clark's answered a knock on her apartment door. A man in his late twenties with "honey-colored" hair stood in the hallway and introduced himself as "Thompson," a painter sent by the building superintendent to paint the ceilings. Without waiting for an invitation, the man walked into the apartment and directly to the bathroom, saying, "We'll have to fix that bathroom ceiling." Then he said, "You know, you have a beautiful figure. Have you ever thought of modeling?" Thinking fast, the woman said her husband was asleep in the bedroom. "Maybe I have the wrong apartment," the man said, and quickly left.

The woman helped police artists make a composite drawing of "Thompson," and several other residents of the building claimed to recognize him. Further investigation revealed that local police officers knew the man as a cab driver who often cruised the neighborhood.

The second suspect police were eager to pick up was a Cambridge minister's son wanted for breaking and entering and assault. Police also were interested in identifying the person who was behind a series of racial incidents aimed at Clark's roommates: might he be linked to the murder? For more than a year Clark's roommates, Audri Adams and Gloria Todd, had been receiving obscene phone calls and vulgar letters threatening them with rape and violence. And on one occasion, someone slit open the convertible top on Adams's car and painted the initials KKK on the door to her apartment. (After this incident, Adams had moved to the safety of Clark's apartment.)

Three weeks later, on New Year's Eve, twenty-three-year-old Patricia Bissette was found dead in her locked apartment. It was in the same Back Bay area where Slesers and Clark had been murdered and where fifty uniformed and plainclothes officers cruised day and night. Bissette had been strangled with items of her clothing: a blouse and several stockings. She was faceup in bed, with the sheet and blanket carefully smoothed and pulled neatly up under her chin. In the living room next to a Christmas tree, police found three buttons from her housecoat, which led them to conclude that the young woman had been murdered there and carried to her bedroom. The medical examiner found evidence that Bissette had recently had sexual intercourse and that she was one month pregnant. Her clothing and personal effects had been disturbed. There was no sign of a forced entry.

The building janitor had seen Bissette on her way to the basement laundry room two days before, a Saturday. An hour or so later when he passed through the room, he noticed that all the machines were empty. He assumed Bissette had picked up her laundry and returned to her apartment. On Monday morning, after Bissette didn't show up for her ride to work, a coworker notified the building janitor, and the two men climbed in the window of Bissette's apartment and made the grisly discovery.

While there were striking similarities between Bissette's murder and that of the other women who had been strangled, homicide detectives initially believed Bissette may have been murdered by a lover. They found two unwashed cups, one with black coffee and one with coffee with cream, which led them to think Bissette had been murdered by someone she knew. The medical examiner's theory was that when Bissette told her lover she was pregnant and perhaps demanded marriage, a violent fight followed. A moment after he murdered her, the remorseful killer tenderly tucked her into bed.

But Bissette had several boyfriends, and they had alibis. The police had no clues and no suspects. Then, less than a week after Bissette's murder, a sixteen-year-old girl was strangled to death and her body found in a Boston alley. Although two weeks later a fifteen-year-old boy confessed to killing her, the heat was now really on the police. Reporters besieged Commissioner McNamara. "What more can we do?" he asked plaintively when reporters demanded to know if he was closer to arresting the Strangler. He had assigned every police officer in the department to hunt for the killer. Police had checked the records of thousands of sex offenders, questioned hundreds of men, and investigated thousands of anonymous telephone tips. But the "persons responsible" were still at large. McNamara believed there were too many "dissimilarities" between the murders—that it wasn't possible to be sure that only one man had murdered all seven women. He refused to elaborate.

The national press began to cover the Boston stranglings. In the February 15, 1963, issue of *LIFE* magazine, six weeks after Bissette's murder, an article entitled "Fear Walks Home with the Women," told how difficult "mass suspicion which bordered on hysteria" had made the Boston police's efforts to find the killer. Boston-area women rushed to locksmiths, purchased dogs, propped makeshift weapons near their beds, and were so fearful of being alone that they were spending weekends with girlfriends or even their parents. The ring of a doorbell was no longer the cheery signal of friends, but a "trigger of alarm." "When

I hear the bell or a knock on the door," one young woman was quoted as saying, "I panic." Another young woman told of circling the block before entering her apartment and then looking immediately in the closets. "The whole thing affects your imagination," she said.

WHAT WAS A GRIPPINGLY COLD WINTER turned to spring, and no other strangling took place. But no one in Boston dared breathe a sigh of relief. And then, on the evening of Sunday, May 5, some time after eleven o'clock, twenty-three-year-old Beverly Samans, a budding opera singer, was murdered in her Cambridge apartment, one block from Harvard Square. A mutual friend had alerted Samans's boyfriend, Oliver Chamberlin Jr., that Beverly had not shown up for choir practice or to a rehearsal for *Cosi fan tutti*. Chamberlin knocked loudly and then used his key to open the door. He saw Samans's body immediately. She lay nude, sprawled on her convertible sofa bed in the living room-bedroom. She had been gagged, her wrists tied behind her. A stocking and two handkerchiefs knotted together were around her neck, but they were mere decoration. The press reported the medical examiner's ruling, that Samans had died as a result of multiple stab wounds to her neck and chest. In fact, the medical examiner's report described eighteen stab wounds making a bull's-eye design around Samans's left breast. Police recovered a bloody knife from the kitchen sink.

Samans had been last seen alive quite late on the day of her murder. Her neighbors heard her practicing arias in the morning, and later that day she sang in the choir of the Second Unitarian Church. In the afternoon and evening she rehearsed for her role in *Cosi fan tutti* until nine o'clock, and then she drove home and met a friend in Cambridge for a late-night snack. It was close to eleven o'clock when they parted company.

Although the use of a knife as a murder weapon distinguished Samans's death from the murders of the other strangling victims, there were important similarities. Samans lived alone and there was no evidence of a forced entry. Like the others, she had connections to music and to medicine. She had planned to audition for the New York Metropolitan Opera Company and she had nearly completed a master's degree in rehabilitation counseling at Boston University. In fact, at the time of her death Samans worked as a counselor at Medfield State Hospital, a mental institution. As with several of the other murders, Samans's body had been placed in a highly visible and shocking position, perhaps to taunt the police. And most agonizing of all, the police had not uncovered a single clue as to the murderer's identity.

There were no new murders bearing the Strangler's trademarks during the summer of 1963. Boston police used the respite to review their evidence once again while other news dominated the headlines: The NAACP announced it intended to picket the Boston School Committee's headquarters, because almost a decade after the Supreme Court's decision in Brown v. Board of Education the committee had done little or nothing about integrating the city's schools. Concern about civil rights also occupied President John F. Kennedy's attention, as did mounting American casualties in Vietnam.

Then, on Sunday, September 8, almost the anniversary of the strangling deaths of Ida Irga and Jane Sullivan, neighbors called police to 224 Lafayette Street in Salem, the first-floor apartment of fifty-eight-year-old Evelyn Corbin. She had celebrated her birthday just a few days earlier. Corbin and her neighbor Flora Manchester habitually shared Sunday breakfast together, each still dressed in nightgown and robe. After breakfast, Corbin would dress for church, pausing on her way out to knock on Manchester's door. She also knocked when she returned. On this Sunday, following their usual breakfast, Corbin failed to signal she was leaving the building to attend mass; Manchester grew worried. With another friend at her side, she unlocked her friend's door. Corbin was sprawled across her bed, her right leg dangling above the floor. Two nylon stockings had been pulled tight around her neck and a third tied around her left ankle in an elaborate bow. The front of her bathrobe had been ripped open with such force that three buttons had flown off. Her underpants had been stuffed in her mouth. Police determined that she had been sexually assaulted.

Police later learned that Corbin recently had visited a friend at Salem Hospital and that she was a skilled pianist. Sheet music lay scattered on the floor of her apartment. Asked if Corbin's murder could be linked to Boston's unsolved stranglings, Detective Donovan replied laconically. "The woman's dead. There's a stocking around her neck. That's similarity enough."

On Friday, November 22, 1963, President Kennedy was assassinated. As the nation mourned during that Thanksgiving weekend, a pleasant, quiet woman named Joann Graff, 23, did not show up to teach Sunday school or sing in the choir at her Lutheran church in Lawrence, an hour's drive north of Boston. Worried, her friends went to her apartment and called police when she failed to answer the door.

The police arrived to find yet another "locked-room" murder. They found Graff strangled and with two nylon stockings intertwined with a leg of a pair of tights tied about her neck in a huge bow and with a double half hitch—the Strangler's signature knot. She lay sprawled diagonally across her bed, nude except for a blouse pushed back from her shoulders and up under her armpits. Her right leg dangled over the edge of the bed, a slipper still on her foot. There were teeth marks on her left breast. The door to Graff's bedroom closet was half open and her underclothing scattered about the room. Because the murderer left untouched an envelope with money, Officer Francis O'Connor ruled out robbery as a motive. "This is so similar to the others," District Attorney John P. Burke said, "it's frightening."

Like the other victims, Graff loved music and had at least a tangential connection to the medical world: a designer, she worked for a company located around the block from her apartment and across the street from Lawrence General Hospital.

When the police made their usual circuit asking neighbors if they had seen anything suspicious, Kenneth Rowe, an engineering student at Northeastern University, volunteered that shortly before 3:30 P.M. on Friday, he had heard footsteps in the hallway. He moved quietly to the door and listened as someone knocked on the door of the apartment directly across the hall. No one answered. A person then knocked on Rowe's door. He opened it and saw a man in his late twenties with dark hair, wearing a brown jacket and dark green trousers. With his hand held midway on his nose and covering his mouth, he asked, "Does Joann Graff live here?" No, Rowe said; she lived in the apartment below. He listened as the stranger walked down the stairs, and a moment later he heard a door on the floor below open and shut.

Rowe's glimpse of the stranger proved too sketchy to be useful, and the police found themselves with nothing to go on. Boston detectives Donovan and Sherry added the latest bunch of questionnaires gathered from Graff's neighbors to a huge pile they had accumulated over the previous seventeen months. They added a picture of Graff and other details of her habits to a bulletin board kept at their office, and they combed through the records of cabdrivers who may have picked up or dropped off a passenger near the apartment of one of the murder victims. And once again they supervised the pickup of dozens of sexual offenders. The two detectives were the point men of a huge ongoing police effort that so far had yielded not a single solid clue. They waited.

Pamela Parker and Patricia Delmore walked home from work in a light snow on Saturday, January 4, 1964, at about six o'clock. The two young women shared a second-floor apartment on Charles Street in Boston with nineteen-year-old Mary Sullivan. Parker rang the bell, but when Mary didn't answer, Delmore used her key to enter the apartment. Believing Mary was asleep, the two women quietly prepared supper and called to Mary to join them. Parker pushed open the door of Sullivan's

Edward W. Brooke III, attorney general of Massachusetts (1963–1967), was the first African-American to hold that office in the United States. In January 1964, he took control of the investigations into all Boston-area stranglings. (**Boston Globe**)

bedroom and saw that her roommate was dead. She shouted, "My God, she's dead! She's been raped. Get the police!" The two young women ran into the street screaming for help. Officer John Vadeboncour heard the young women's cries for help, ran up the stairs, took one look at the body, and called for homicide detectives. Among other police officers, Detective Donovan rushed to the scene, which was already crowded with four hundred or five hundred curious onlookers. During the uproar, William Ivey, a Boston University student engaged to Delmore, arrived at the scene. He told police the girls had complained about a defective kitchen window and that someone had been on the fire escape a few nights earlier.

While a uniformed officer listened to Ivey, Donovan climbed the stairs to the women's apartment. He found Sullivan's body propped up on a bed, her back against the headboard, her buttocks on a pillow, her knees up. A broomstick had been inserted into her vagina. There were semen stains on the blanket. A stocking and two scarves were knotted around Sullivan's neck, the last tied loosely in a big floppy bow. Against her left foot the killer had placed a brightly colored New Year's card. Captain Cornelius O'Brien said the murder had "the earmarks of some of the others." He also noted that a previous victim, Ida Irga, had lived on Grove Street, five blocks from Sullivan's apartment.

Two weeks after Mary Sullivan's death, Massachusetts Attorney General Edward W. Brooke III announced that he was assuming total control of the investigation into the stranglings.

CHAPTER THREE

The Hunt for the Strangler(s)

Mary Sullivan's murder was the eleventh unsolved strangling in eighteen months. Something about her death seemed to strike people particularly hard: she was young, happy-go-lucky, optimistic, and eager—in fact, she looked like every young woman bent on making it in Boston—and her brutal death came right on the heels of the Christmas holidays. Whether there was one madman or more on the loose, it was very clear that women of all ages were the targets.

"We start now," Attorney General Brooke said on January 17, 1964, as he announced the creation of the Special Division of Crime and Research Detection, or as it was popularly known, the Strangler Bureau. Handsome, intelligent, and polished, the forty-four-year-old Brooke was the only African-American attorney general in the United States. A World War II veteran and a Republican in a solidly Democratic state, the Howard University and Boston University Law School graduate had swept into office in 1963.

Brooke was keenly aware that assuming control of the Strangler investigation carried considerable political risk. "I know I can be criticized by both police and public," he admitted. But, he pointed out, this was an "abnormal case and an unusual case and it demands abnormal and unusual procedures." He had no disrespect for the Boston police, but the fact that the killings spanned five different police jurisdictions cried out for coordination and consistency by experts whose only job was to find and bring to justice the person or persons terrorizing the city. The Strangler Bureau was intended to end the all-too-common practice of one police department withholding information from another because of petty jealousies or feuds or because one department assumed the murders were not related.

Brooke chose his long-time friend and B.U. Law School classmate, John S. Bottomly, to head the bureau. As head of the attorney general's forty-four-person Eminent Domain Department, Bottomly oversaw complex negotiations involving the state's taking of thousands of pieces of property to make way for urban renewal and new highways. In his first year on the job, he successfully disposed of cases that had been on the court's docket for over a decade. In appointing him to head the Strangler Bureau, Brooke praised Bottomly's superb organizational skills and enthusiasm for new challenges.

John S. Bottomly, an assistant attorney general, was appointed coordinator of the Strangler Bureau in January 1964. He abruptly resigned the position on the eve of DeSalvo's sexual assault trial. (**Boston Globe**)

Still, with no experience in criminal law, and as a Republican in the very Democratic city of Boston, Bottomly was a controversial choice. When Police Commissioner McNamara heard about the appointment, he allegedly said, "Holy Jesus, what a nut cake." George Higgins, a Boston-based reporter later turned novelist, said he never heard a flattering reference to Bottomly.

Bottomly's team consisted of Boston Police Detective Phillip DiNatale, State Police Detective Andrew Tuney, Special Officer James Mellon, and Metropolitan Police Officer Stephen Delaney. Dr. Donald Kenefick, a Boston University psychiatrist, headed the six-man Medical-Psychiatric Committee. (The only women involved on the team were administrative secretary Jane Downey and clerical assistant Sandra Irizarry.) Brooke later added the well-known Dutch psychic Peter Hurkos. To prevent media criticism, Bottomly withheld Hurkos's involvement from the public and arranged for an anonymous Boston industrialist to pay the psychic's salary.

Before beginning its investigative work, the Strangler Bureau had to collect, organize, and assimilate more than 37,000 pages of information that the Boston police had collected. The data was organized into casebooks, one for each unsolved strangling. Multiple copies of each casebook were made and distributed to each investigator and consultant. Each investigator would focus on the details—the victim's background, friends, habits, work, church, likes and dislikes. They hoped to find a link joining the victims and ultimately limit the number of possible suspects.

Bottomly turned to a Concord computing firm to accelerate and refine this process. Working with the director of the Massachusetts Bureau of Identification, the firm created a massive number of key-punch cards, each containing a specific piece of data to be fed into a computer. The computer could then sort out the characteristics the victims shared or identify suspects who had contact with one or more of the victims.

Even with this latest computer technology, charting each victim's every move was a huge task. Equally daunting was the list of possible suspects. Nearly five hundred sex offenders had been released from the state's jails in 1963, and they were only part of the pool of possible perpetrators: the murderer might not have a criminal record, or might be a mentally disturbed man with a history of violence or the potential for violent behavior. And of course there might be more than one murderer.

New York City Public Health Commissioner James Brussel, who had created a remarkably accurate profile of New York's "Mad Bomber," a disgruntled former Consolidated Edison employee who had sought revenge against the company by setting off explosive devices, told two Boston reporters that he had developed a profile of the Strangler. He would, Brussel said, be built like a ballet dancer, powerful and compact. He argued that the Strangler was not fixated on older women, but that younger women could satisfy his psychological need as well. Further, he speculated that the Strangler found murdering women to be therapeutic, but that if he could sexually assault a young woman before she was dead or unconscious, he might be able to stop killing altogether.

Dr. Kenefick and his Medical-Psychological Committee disagreed with Brussel's profile of the killer. They had a different theory. They believed that one man, the Strangler, probably had murdered the five older women as a psychotic expression of hatred for his mother but that one or more men—copycats—had murdered the young women. They believed the murderers would be found among the young women's circle of acquaintances, most likely "unstable members of the homosexual community" who made their murderous acts look like the Strangler's work. Kenefick's committee cited evidence that homosexuals frequented the Beacon Hill and the Back Bay areas where Sophie Clark and Mary Sullivan lived, and that Beverly Samans lived just a block from Harvard Square, an area notorious for eccentric characters, and that she had been writing a thesis on homosexuality. The Kenefick group even stretched their hypothesis to include Joann Graff, because they assumed that many of the men she met in her line of work—artistic design— were gay. No one questioned or even tried to present evidence to support the assumption that homosexual men were more prone to violence than heterosexual men.

Kenefick theorized that the murderer would not act oddly; rather, he would appear pleasant, gentle, and compassionate and would move easily among his fellow workers and acquaintances. But all the time he would barely be able to contain within himself "an encapsulated core of rage" that could explode at any time and usually would be directed at a dominant, powerful female, usually someone like his mother. Life's ordinary stresses and disappointments might trigger the rage and cause the homosexual to murder, to destroy the hated female image. But one murder did not solve the homosexual's deep-seated problem. Therefore, he would kill again and again. Each time he killed, Kenefick suggested, he was attempting to "reestablish a seductive scene, to carry out buried incestuous fantasies, and to exorcise certain fears by acting out a fantasy of degrading and controlling an overwhelming and fearsome mother." He left his victims in shocking poses not only to degrade them, but also to suggest that they had tried to seduce him.

The Medical-Psychological Committee members pondered why no one had been murdered since Mary Sullivan. Several speculated that the Strangler might have committed suicide, succumbing to a rage that could be satisfied only by taking his own life. Others suggested that he may have been arrested for another crime or that he was lying low until the investigation lost its steam. In an interview on August 19, 1964, Brooke said he doubted that the "mad strangler" was still on the streets, and like the psychiatrists, he suggested that "unstable homosexuals" were responsible for murdering the six young women.

As Brooke's remark made clear, Kenefick's profile largely shaped the investigation. It did not, however, lead police to any specific suspects. State Police detective Andrew Tuney, for example, was eager to test the validity of the psychiatric profile. He spent nights writing down the license plate numbers of cars parked near Boston clubs frequented by homosexuals. With the names of the car owners in hand, Tuney hoped to link them with the names of gay men with whom the murder victims may have had contact. He also sought to use the information to identify what he called the "homosexual hierarchy" and to learn who members of this elite talked to and what names they mentioned in their conversations. Tuney wanted information that would justify wiretapping this alleged leadership group. No such information surfaced.

The Strangler Bureau team also followed every lead that might connect mental patients with a history of sexual assault to the murders. In May 1963, police detective DiNatale had met with Paul Gordon, an advertising copywriter in his early forties who allegedly had extrasensory perception (ESP). Gordon claimed his ESP had revealed that the Strangler was a mental patient he could name. Gordon and DiNatale met near one of the victim's apartments, and Gordon articulated details about the murders that had not appeared in newspapers. DiNatale was interested but remained skeptical.

Nearly a year later, John Bottomly revived interest in Gordon. The Bureau chief contacted a Tufts Medical School psychiatrist who, with Gordon's permission, administered a hypnotic drug. Bottomly wanted to eliminate Gordon as a suspect—how did he know details about the murders if he was not the murderer?—or be convinced that the mental patient Gordon had identified, who now sat silently staring at a blank wall in Bridgewater State Hospital was, in fact, the Strangler. For six hours, DiNatale and officer Jim Mellon listened intently while Gordon talked and answered questions as communicated to him through ESP from the mental patient. At the end of the session Bottomly was certain that neither Gordon nor the mental patient was the Strangler.

Other suspects came to police attention the old-fashioned way. Daniel J. Pennacchio, a busboy working in a Cambridge cafeteria, confessed to murdering Beverly Samans, the eighth victim. Pennacchio had been arrested when nurses at nearby Mount Auburn Hospital found him lying on the floor outside the ladies' restroom, peeping under the door. Police quickly discovered he had recently been discharged from the Fernald State School (a school for mentally retarded children), where Samans had taught. Detectives were about to interrogate Pennacchio when he blurted out, "All right, I'll tell you everything. I did it." He told police he had knocked on Samans's apartment door about midnight of May 5. She had let him in and they talked while she typed her thesis. When asked, "Did you stab Beverly Samans?" Pennacchio said yes. Thirty minutes later, he signed a confession.

Cambridge police booked Pennacchio for murder, but Judge Edward Viola refused to issue a murder complaint, because some of Pennacchio's answers were not consistent with the facts known to police. His lawyer told the court that Pennacchio was mentally retarded and eager to please the officers by giving answers he thought they wanted to hear. He was held on the original charge of lewd and lascivious behavior.

Without pausing, the Bureau team turned to other suspects. Officer Mellon and detective DiNatale suspected that Lewis Barnett, a friend of Sophie Clark's, had not given full and honest answers to their questions, but when they went looking for him, he had disappeared. He had quit his job and had left his Boston apartment without leaving a forwarding address. Eventually, in May 1964, Mellon and DiNatale found him in New York City. When they asked him why he had run, Barnett told the detectives that Clark's death had affected him profoundly and he could not bear to live in Boston.

Barnett told Mellon and DiNatale that he had been alone with Clark only once, on Saturday, December 1, four days before her murder.

Clark's roommates had said that in fact Barnett had visited Clark several other times. Barnett insisted that on the night of Clark's murder he had come home from work, taken a nap, grabbed a bite to eat, and taken out another young woman. To clarify the discrepancy about how many times he had visited Clark and to verify his alibi, Mellon and DiNatale asked Barnett to take a lie detector test. He agreed.

The polygraph test was administered in New York City. The examiner asked ten questions, including "Were you in the apartment at the time that death came to Sophie Clark?" To that question Barnett answered no. According to the polygraph, Barnett lied. In different order, the operator repeated the same ten questions. The needles charting Barnett's responses jumped again when asked if he witnessed Clark's murder. "Lew, you're lying," the examiner said. Barnett jumped up, cursed, and demanded the wires be removed from his arms.

The failed polygraph test was not sufficient evidence (the results were inadmissible in court) to arrest Barnett. But during the drive to Barnett's Harlem apartment, DiNatale told Barnett he had better pack a bag, because he was going to away for a long time. "If I was the guy who did it, would I get the electric chair?" Barnett asked. "No, of course not," DiNatale answered. "They don't do that if you're sick. They take you and put you in a hospital and give you the best of care until you're cured and then they let you go." DiNatale thought Barnett was on the verge of confessing. But then he stopped talking. When the car came to halt in front of his apartment, Barnett practically jumped out of the car.

A week later DiNatale surprised Barnett as he stood drinking at a New York bar. If you're truly innocent, DiNatale said, come back to Boston now and clear this up once and for all. Barnett agreed. The Boston polygraph test results were inconclusive, though the examiner believed Barnett was hiding something. Again, DiNatale challenged Barnett, this time getting the young man to agree to speak to a psychiatrist while under the sway of a hypnotic drug.

Following some casual conversation, Barnett acknowledged that he was bisexual and that at the time of Clark's murder he lived with a young male hairdresser. He began to cry. Speaking between loud sobs, Barnett said he felt responsible for Clark's death. He had thought about dropping by to see her on the afternoon of her murder, but he decided to stay home because of the bad weather. "If only I'd been there," he said, "I'd have protected her." He acted as if he were conscience-stricken. DiNatale was not so sure he believed Barnett, but there was nothing he could do unless, and until, new evidence incriminating Barnett turned up

Meanwhile, the Boston media kept up its drumbeat. As a spring 1964 issue of *LIFE* put it, Boston's "hyperthyroid newspapers seldom let anyone forget, the city of Boston and the communities around it have been afflicted with 11 stranglings since June 1962." Without doubt, equal doses of media hype, criticism, and desperation led the bureau team to turn to Peter Hurkos, a famous Dutch psychic who supposedly developed extrasensory powers after falling from a ladder onto his head, lapsing into a coma, and regaining consciousness. With his newly acquired "psychometrics" technique, he saw pictures as he touched objects, "like on TV," he said. "They come and go in my brain. They show me what I'm looking for."

Hurkos had already helped find a missing girl in Illinois and fingered a Virginia trash collector as the murderer of a family of four. Though the trash man eventually proved to be innocent, Hurkos insisted his suspect shared many characteristics with the actual perpetrator. Boston police scoffed at the idea of bringing in the famous seer, but Brooke and Bottomly figured they had nothing to lose. Bureau officers flew him into Providence, Rhode Island, and drove him to Lexington, Massachusetts, to avoid any media coverage.

Bottomly assigned a bright, young assistant attorney general named Julian Soshnick to work with Hurkos. The day after his arrival, Hurkos, his bodyguard, Soshnick, Sergeant Leo Martin, and a police stenographer to record the conversations, crowded around a bed in a Lexington motel room on which Soshnick had placed more than a dozen piles of photographs facedown. Hurkos, a heavy-set, jowly man with black eyes, bent over the bed and ran his finger back and forth over the several piles. Suddenly he slammed his hand down on one pile. "Phony baloney," he cried. He was right; the pile contained pictures of a murder the police had solved already.

Hurkos began to gaze intently at the other piles of photographs. "Every victim lay different," he said with a heavy Dutch accent. He lay on the floor near the bed and demonstrated how the Strangler had arranged each victim. Each time the photos corroborated the pose Hurkos struck.

Next he took the stockings, scarves, and blouses the Strangler had tied around the necks of his victims. He rubbed each piece carefully, using what he called his "radar brain" to conjure an image of the murderer. He's not too big, he said, between five feet seven and five feet eight, and in a flash he made a mark on the motel wall at about that height. The man weighed between 130 and 140 pounds, had a sharp nose, a scar on his left arm from an industrial accident, and a deformed thumb. He worked as a door-to-door shoe salesman, selling nurses' shoes. Now Hurkos described a scene moving through his head: "I see man—he come from hospital, then down basement—he with stick, he use stick first to switch around room, then put stick in vagina, and he masturbate."

After supper that night Hurkos continued to describe the pictures moving through his brain. "This man," he said breathing heavily, "he not sleep in bed. No mattress, nothing." Hurkos spoke quickly, in sentence fragments. "Not a colored man. White." A short pause, then, "He love shoes!" "He look in suitcase not for money but for shoes." "Maybe he masturbate in shoes." Speaking faster, Hurkos said, "When he kill her, she must have shoes on. But he must be clean to God. God walks barefoot." Further, "After killing he sleep like God sleep, on iron, on steel, on pins."

Hurkos asked for a local map. He drew a circle around an area in Newton, including Boston College. "I see this man here," Hurkos said, tapping the penciled circle he had drawn on the map. "He lives in a building with a small window. Not paying rent. Getting free soup." On Friday morning a detective drove Hurkos to the area he had marked on the map. "I see the building with small windows!" he yelled just as they passed St. John's Seminary, near Boston College. As the car drove toward Bottomly's Boston office, Hurkos suddenly shouted again, "There's been a murder here!" In fact, they had just driven past 1940 Commonwealth Avenue, where Nina Nichols had lived.

That evening, when they had returned to the Lexington motel, Hurkos instructed the police stenographer and an officer with a tape recorder to sit by his bed, because he often talked in his sleep. During the next four hours Hurkos did talk while he slept. Among other fascinating bits and pieces of conversations, he began a debate between himself and the killer, who spoke in a soft, effeminate voice with a Boston accent. The killer said "the monks" had not liked him. Hurkos finally fell silent and slept peacefully.

Before Hurkos arrived on the scene, the Strangler Bureau had received a letter forwarded from the dean of the School of Nursing at Boston College. The letter was from a man claiming to be an alumnus, and a professional writer. He proposed writing an article about the school's 1950 graduates. Further, he was interested in meeting a young female nurse so that "we could begin a friendship that might lead to the altar." A police officer checked the name used by the letter writer against a master list of Strangler suspects. There was a match: months before, the Bureau had received an anonymous letter suggesting that a man of that name was the killer. Bottomly ordered a check on the man's description and background which by coincidence he received while Hurkos was in Boston.

The detectives assigned to Hurkos were astonished. The letter writer's description matched perfectly the verbal sketch of the killer Hurkos had given when he touched the strangler's victims' stockings. First, the letter writer had a history of mental illness. Second, he was five feet eight inches tall, weighed 125 pounds, had a sharp nose, and a scar on his arm. Third, the man had entered St. John's Seminary in order to become a Catholic priest, but he had quit because the discipline was too tough. ("The monks" had not liked him.) And, fourth, he had sold nurses' shoes. But was he the killer?

Bottomly first tried to have the man voluntarily commit himself for psychiatric observation, but when Bureau officers spoke to him at his Back Bay apartment, he refused their suggestion. Next, Bottomly made use of an old Massachusetts law permitting a police officer or a doctor to put anyone "showing derangement other than drunkenness" into an institution for ten days' observation. Police returned with a court order. "I guess I'm in trouble," the shoe salesman said, and he went along quietly to the Fernwood Road Mental Health Institution.

A few days later, police showed the letter writer photos of the Strangler's victims, thinking he might be shocked into confessing. But he had no visible reaction and said nothing. Without a confession, or evidence tying the troubled shoe salesman to the murders, the police concluded he was not the killer. The next day Boston newspapers learned of the man's detention and that he had been identified as the Strangler by Hurkos.

At this point everything came apart. Hurkos was arrested in New York City for impersonating an FBI agent. He said it was all a misunderstanding, and a U.S. Commissioner released Hurkos on $2,500 bail. In Boston, a young civil rights attorney publicly charged the attorney general with misusing the mentally ill commitment statute to hold the shoe salesman rather than bringing a criminal charge. New evidence showed the salesman had ironclad alibis on the dates of the murders, and Brooke released the state's hold on the troubled mental patient.

The hot summer of 1964 slowly gave way to cool fall days. Labor Day marked eight months since the last strangling. The Strangler Bureau had accumulated a vast amount of information about each of the victims, but was no closer to identifying a viable suspect or to making an arrest than when the murderous spree began in June 1962. Then, several months later, Cambridge police made an arrest that would signal the beginning of the end of the fear.

CHAPTER FOUR

Albert DeSalvo and F. Lee Bailey

On the morning of October 27, 1964, a few minutes after nine-thirty, a twenty-year-old recently married Cambridge woman lay half-asleep in her bed. Her husband had just left for his teaching job. She nodded off to sleep but awoke to see a strange man standing in her bedroom. "Don't worry," he said as he moved toward her. She shot back, "You leave this room at once," and moved to get up. She was too slow. He had reached her bedside.

The man shoved her down, and she felt a knife blade against her throat. "Not a sound, or I'll kill you," he growled. Moving quickly, he stuffed her underwear into her mouth. Grabbing her husband's pajamas and some of her clothing, he tied her to the bed in a spread-eagle position. He kissed her body and sexually abused her, repeatedly warning, "Don't look at me!" Finally he asked, "How do I leave this place?" Somehow, she managed to direct him to the front door. Turning his face away from her, he bent over the bed and loosened the knotted clothing that held her prisoner. "You be quiet for ten minutes," he said. Then, before he vanished, he said, "I'm sorry."

The brave young woman had looked at her assailant's face, and she helped a police artist produce a sketch of a man with dark hair slicked back pompadour style, dark eyes, and a "Jimmy Durante" nose. (The police sketch was similar to Peter Hurkos's description of the Strangler.) A Cambridge detective immediately recognized the man depicted in the portrait as Albert DeSalvo, a con man who in 1960 and 1961 had fast-talked dozens of young women into allowing him to measure their height, hips, waist, bust, and legs, by claiming he was going to get them into modeling. Police, cruising a neighborhood where a series of house-breaks had occurred, had arrested "the Measuring Man," as he was known, on March 17, 1961, after a chase through Cambridge back-yards. DeSalvo had dropped a long-handled screwdriver, the favorite tool of housebreakers. In his parked car were four more such tools. DeSalvo admitted he had tried to break into a Cambridge apartment where he knew two nurses lived. "I just wanted to wait for them to come home," he told a detective at the Cambridge police station.

Following a psychiatric examination at Westborough State Hospital, the court sentenced DeSalvo to a two-year term for assault and battery and attempted breaking and entering. He was found not guilty of two counts of lewdness. He eventually served only eleven months before being released in April 1962. As far as the Cambridge police knew, DeSalvo had stayed out of trouble until the reported sexual assault in October 1964.

At that time, police asked DeSalvo to come to police headquarters. He denied any knowledge of the sexual assault, but the young victim—watching through a one-way mirror and listening through a partially open door—positively identified him as her assailant. He pleaded innocent to the charges, posted bail, and was released pending a scheduled hearing.

In the meantime, according to usual police practice, DeSalvo's photograph went out to a regional network. Within hours, Connecticut police responded. They had been hunting for a man—known colloquially as the "Green Man" because he wore green work pants—who had carried out a string of similar sexual assaults in a number of Connecticut cities and towns in the summer of 1964. Acting on this new information, Cambridge police arrested DeSalvo again. Several women victims from Connecticut identified him in a lineup.

Confronted with these new accusations, DeSalvo insisted on talking with his wife, Irmgard. In the presence of detectives, the couple talked for nearly an hour. Albert begged his wife, a tall, dark-haired

Dr. Ames Robey (right), medical director at Bridgewater State Hospital from 1963 to 1966, testified that DeSalvo was competent to stand trial for sexual assault. Donald L. Conn (left), assistant district attorney, Middlesex County, argued that DeSalvo was competent to stand trial and successfully prosecuted him for sexual assault. **(Boston Globe)**

woman of thirty, to let him tell everything he had done. "Al, tell them everything, don't hold anything back," she said and left. He confessed to hundreds of Boston-area housebreaks and to the sexual assaults of hundreds of women throughout New England. And, he added almost casually, "There's a couple of rapes you don't know about."

Sensing they might have the Strangler on their hands, Sergeant Leo Davenport asked DeSalvo about the stranglings. He emphatically denied ever murdering anyone. Come to think of it, Davenport noted, DeSalvo didn't fit the Bureau's psychological profile of the Strangler. He was not a homosexual; he was not consumed with rage; he did not hate his mother; and if he was to be believed, he certainly had no problem with sexual potency.

DeSalvo appeared in court the day following his astonishing confession, and a judge ordered him to Bridgewater State Hospital for pretrial observation. Dr. Ames Robey, a Boston University Medical School graduate who had trained with Dr. Donald Kenefick, head of the Strangler Bureau's Medical-Psychological Committee, reported that De-Salvo suffered from a "sociopathic personality disorder marked by sexual deviation, with prominent schizoid features and depressive trends." Nevertheless, Robey said De-Salvo was competent to stand trial for sexual assault. Awaiting trial in Cambridge, however, DeSalvo began to act very strangely and was returned to

F. Lee Bailey was the brilliant young Boston attorney who represented DeSalvo. (Boston Globe)

Bridgewater for additional testing. This time staff psychiatrists concluded that he was not competent to stand trial. On February 4, 1965, the Middlesex Superior Court ordered him held at Bridgewater for treatment until further order of the court.

A few days later, a murder suspect, George Nassar, arrived at Bridgewater for psychiatric observation. Described by a psychiatrist as "very paranoid, very bright, very angry," Nassar had been charged with an especially brutal and senseless murder. He had been identified as the man who, late in the afternoon of September 29, 1964, murdered a gas station attendant, firing six shots at point-blank range into the man's head and body.

Police knew Nassar; he had served eleven years in prison for the shooting death of a grocery-store clerk. He seemed rehabilitated and was paroled in 1962. After his release Nassar taught Sunday school and studied Russian. He was extremely bright, with an IQ above 150. He had held several jobs, including a stint as a hospital attendant, as he prepared to take classes at Northeastern University. Now, two years after his release, he was charged with murder again and sent to Bridgewater for psychiatric evaluation. There he befriended Albert DeSalvo.

Despite his earlier statement that he had never committed a murder, DeSalvo confided to Nassar that he was the Boston Strangler. Nassar told his attorney. The attorney was F. Lee Bailey. Bailey wasted no time in learning about DeSalvo. Later that same day, he asked Dr. Ames Robey, the chief psychiatrist at Bridgewater, if he knew DeSalvo. "I know Albert very well," he told Bailey. "If you believe one-tenth of what he says, he has the strongest sexual drive in the history of the United States. But I'm afraid most of it is fantasy." Withholding the information Nassar had given him, Bailey asked Robey if DeSalvo might be homicidal. "I don't think Albert could kill anybody if his mother's life depended upon it," Robey said.

A week later DeSalvo's brother, Joseph, called Bailey's office to report that Albert wanted to see Bailey. In preparation for the meeting, Bailey told Boston homicide detective John Donovan that he might be talking to a man who claimed to have committed some of the stranglings. So that he might judge the man's credibility, Bailey asked Donovan to divulge some information about the stranglings that police had not revealed to the public. According to Bailey's memoir, *The Defense Never Rests*, Donovan provided with him some information, and on March 4, 1965, Bailey went to Bridgewater to meet DeSalvo.

Although he was just shy of his thirty-third birthday when he signed in to talk to DeSalvo, Bailey stood on the threshold of becoming a nationally known criminal attorney. Born in Waltham, Massachusetts, Bailey attended a New Hampshire prep school and entered Harvard College at the age of sixteen. He left before graduating to join the United States Marines. From 1952 to 1956 he served as a Marine fighter pilot and chief legal officer for a Marine unit based in North Carolina. After his discharge, he enrolled at Boston University Law School and worked as an investigator for a Boston lawyer. Just three months after he was admitted to the Massachusetts bar in 1960, Bailey won his first murder case. Less than a year later he became the attorney for Sam Sheppard, a Cleveland, Ohio, doctor who had been convicted of murdering his pregnant wife in 1954. Sheppard claimed he had come home, surprised his wife's killer, and was knocked unconscious by the "bushy-haired" intruder after a struggle. The prosecution argued that Sheppard murdered his wife because she discovered he was having an affair. Free to read lurid newspaper stories about Sheppard's private life while the trial was in progress, the jury found him guilty. Bailey ultimately won a reversal from the Supreme Court of the United States and became a national celebrity.

Nassar introduced Bailey to DeSalvo in one of the small rooms at Bridgewater reserved for attorney-client meetings. Bailey warned DeSalvo that because Nassar was present, he did not enjoy the benefits of attorney-client privilege. Therefore, he warned him not to refer specifically to any criminal acts he may have committed. For that reason, DeSalvo spoke hypothetically. "If a man had done some terrible things, and if he were sick and wanted to make these things known so that he could get better help and maybe be some good to society, could a lawyer help him do that?" It would be difficult, Bailey replied, but it could be done. "Well, that's what I really want," DeSalvo said. Bailey asked why he had decided to come forward now, and DeSalvo said it was for his family. He had a seven-year-old daughter and a two-year-old son, and he hoped that by selling his story he could provide them with money. Bailey suggested that there were problems about confessing in print to a crime that had not come to trial. But, he told DeSalvo, there could be a way for you to tell your story and to get the help you want without "causing your execution." Toward the end of their meeting, Bailey asked DeSalvo some questions, based on information he had received from Donovan. Bailey recognized that he could not determine the validity of DeSalvo's answers, but he came away "impressed by the speed with which [DeSalvo] responded"—and by the fact that he seemed to be "recalling scenes he had actually experienced."

DESALVO ALSO TALKED ABOUT HIS CHILDHOOD, his army service, and his sexual behavior before he turned murderous. Albert was the third of six children born to Frank and Charlotte DeSalvo. The family lived in a walk-up tenement in Chelsea, a Boston working-class suburb. Frank worked sporadically, drank heavily, and beat Charlotte and the children. On one occasion, when Albert was seven, he watched his father slug his mother in the mouth, knocking out several of her teeth, and then bend back every one of her fingers until they broke. Another time, Frank sold

Albert and his two sisters to a Maine farmer, and Charlotte didn't find the children for six months. Frank eventually abandoned his family, though he came back from time to time on drunken rampages to smash things and beat up whoever was unlucky enough to be in his path. At the conclusion of one of these tirades, Albert, then eight, chased after his father and threw a glass vase at him. In 1944, when Albert was thirteen, Charlotte finally divorced Frank.

Before the divorce, Frank DeSalvo had taught his son the art of shoplifting. At age twelve Albert and a friend beat up a local newsboy and robbed him of $2.85. The court suspended the sentence. But later, he and his buddy were caught breaking into a house and stealing jewelry. Just after Christmas 1943, Albert was sent to the Lyman School for Boys, a reform school, where he spent ten months. (His brother Joseph also had spent time at the Lyman School.) Upon his release, Albert struggled in school; a test showed he had an IQ of 93.

Bailey learned that Albert had become acquainted with sex at an early age. His father brought prostitutes into their Chelsea home, and Albert was "tutored" in sexual techniques by an older woman neighbor. The summer he graduated from junior high school, at age sixteen, he worked at a Cape Cod motel, where he spent free time on the roof peeking into guest rooms and masturbating.

Albert joined the army two weeks after his seventeenth birthday. Following basic training, he was sent to Germany, where he served as a military policeman. In August 1950 he was court-martialed and fined for refusing to obey an order, but after that his record was good. He won promotion to sergeant and became the army's middleweight boxing champion in Europe. He met and later married Irmgard Beck, a young German woman who lived with her parents near Frankfurt. (He later admitted to being sexually active in Germany before his marriage and during a 1959 vacation trip to visit Irmgard's parents.) Four months after their marriage, in April 1954, Albert and Irmgard came to the United States, and for the next twenty-two months— until Albert received an honorable discharge—they lived at Fort Dix, New Jersey.

About a year before DeSalvo's discharge, he was charged with carnal abuse, for sexually molesting a nine-year-old New Jersey girl. The girl's mother had left her three children at home for forty-five minutes while she ran to the grocery store. When she came home, her daughter told her that a soldier had come into the house and touched her on her chest and between her legs. Guided by the girl's description, police arrested DeSalvo, whom they knew from an earlier complaint. DeSalvo vigorously denied the story, and the mother, fearful of bad publicity, refused to press charges. Two months later DeSalvo was reported as a "Peeping Tom" and charged with disorderly conduct. The charges were dropped in both cases, and the army took no action.

A month after these incidents, Irmgard gave birth to the couple's first child, Judy. Irmgard had a lengthy and painful delivery, and Judy's legs were so deformed doctors said she would never walk. In an attempt to correct the deformity, the baby wore a "frog cast," a harness that surrounded the hips and upper legs and was laced into place. Doctors also prescribed physical therapy. Every day Albert fastened Judy into the cast and tied the laces with a big bow. He massaged Judy's legs and slowly moved her legs open and closed. The pain made the child cry. Albert, often in tears also, told Judy he had to hurt her to help her.

Judy's therapy caused problems in the DeSalvos' marriage. Irmgard was so anxious about experiencing the pain of childbirth again or of giving birth to a severely deformed child that she insisted they stop having sexual intercourse altogether. Albert believed she was frigid or that she didn't love him.

In the midst of this marital crisis, the DeSalvos moved back to Chelsea. Albert worked as a press operator for American Biltrite Rubber Company in nearby Everett. Although both he and Irmgard held jobs, they had little money. On Valentine's Day 1958, he broke into a home and stole a cache of silver dollars, several of which were stained with red nail polish. By chance a police officer walked into a candy store just as DeSalvo, buying a valentine for Irmgard and candy for Judy, pushed several of the stained coins across the counter. In court, DeSalvo's lawyer stressed his military service and his need to care for his family, and the judge gave him a suspended sentence.

DeSalvo's tendency to criminality and his compulsive sexual behavior led him to take more chances. At Biltrite he worked either the three-to-eleven or the seven-to-three shift. After leaving work, he would cross the Mystic River Bridge into Boston and quickly select a neighborhood to work his "Measuring Man" scam, touching young women and sometimes having consensual sexual intercourse. Within thirty minutes he would be back on the road, hurrying home to beat the traffic. As he lightheartedly put it, "Bing, bing!" At the same time, he "knew he was getting out of control."

♟   ♟   ♟

ON THE DAY AFTER BAILEY'S INITIAL conversation with DeSalvo, detective DiNatale came to Bridgewater hospital to talk with DeSalvo. Until this point, DeSalvo had been passed over as a possible suspect in the stranglings because his prison records indicated he had been imprisoned for breaking and entering, not for sexual assault. But when the Cambridge police learned about the sexual assaults DeSalvo allegedly committed in Connecticut, they called DiNatale. The detective read DeSalvo's thick file, taking note especially of the fact that he had used nylon stockings to tie up his Connecticut victims. DiNatale also interviewed DeSalvo's former employers and discovered that he had either been off from work or on a shift that gave him the opportunity to commit every one of the brutal murders attributed to the Strangler.

DiNatale hurried to Bridgewater to interview DeSalvo, but when he learned that Bailey was DeSalvo's lawyer, the detective left the hospital. DiNatale knew he could not question a suspect without his lawyer present.

On the following day Bailey recorded his interrogation of DeSalvo, specifically asking him about the stranglings. Two nights later he invited McNamara, Donovan, Sherry, and Dr. Robey to listen to the tape recording of DeSalvo's "confession." Bailey set conditions: the session was only for the purpose of identifying the man Bailey believed was the Strangler; nothing the man said could be used against him; and so that the police could not claim to recognize the voice and then be able to testify against the man later, Bailey varied the playback speed.

The taped conversation made it clear that DeSalvo remembered not only the major outlines of the murders, but also trivial details about the color of a rug or a piece of furniture or a photograph on a dresser in a particular apartment. Although his memory was not perfect, the level of accuracy in his information was extraordinarily high. When, for example, DeSalvo recounted for Bailey his attack on Ida Irga, the fourth victim, he talked first about how he gained access to her apartment. He came to repair a leaky window, he told her, but she was wary. OK, he said, I'll come back tomorrow. When he started to walk away, she said, "Well, come on in." He described the apartment's layout accurately and also correctly recounted that the bed had not been made and that the dresser drawers were empty.

Next, Bailey asked DeSalvo to talk about the murders of Patricia Bissette, Mary Sullivan, and Anna Slesers. DeSalvo said the door of Bissette's apartment opened outward and that she had a black jewelry box on the dresser and Christmas packages on the bed. He added that he had a cup of instant coffee with her. DeSalvo said he gagged Mary Sullivan and placed a sweater over her face. He described the design on her headboard, against which he propped her body. He had left a knife on the bed, he said. He drew a picture of it. He said Slesers lived on the top floor. He recalled hearing classical music and that he turned the volume down all the way, but did not turn off the machine. He got blood on his clothing, so he wore Slesers's raincoat when he left. (Later, from a rack of a dozen women's raincoats the police had assembled, he picked out one identical to Slesers's coat).

DeSalvo said he had not planned any of his assaults. He had no idea who his victims would be. He would drive into a Boston neighborhood and find a place to park. He would walk into a nearby apartment building's lobby and press door buzzers until a woman answered. Whichever woman opened her door first would be his next victim. The so-called Strangler's knot, he said, was not meant to be decorative. It was the kind of knot he had used to hold his daughter's harness in place.

When the tape finished, McNamara lit a cigar and asked, "Well, gentlemen, what do you recommend?" The detectives cautiously suggested administering a lie detector test and checking out the information provided by DeSalvo. Although the detectives felt it was premature to conclude that DeSalvo was the Strangler, they were impressed. A subsequent hypnosis session arranged by Bailey added additional credibility to DeSalvo's claim to be the Strangler. Robey, however, remained unconvinced.

On March 11, 1965, the *Boston Record American* printed a story about the confession without naming DeSalvo. Later that same day,

Attorney General Brooke confirmed that an unnamed inmate at Bridgewater was a key suspect in the Strangler case.

In July 1965, John Bottomly, chief of the Strangler Bureau, announced he would conduct all the further interviews with DeSalvo and Bailey put aside his investigative role. DeSalvo's rights as a mental patient would be carefully protected. None of what he said to Bottomly could be used against him in court. Detectives would not be present— so they could not be subpoenaed to testify—but they would see the transcripts of the sessions so they could check out the accuracy of what DeSalvo said. If they determined that DeSalvo was telling the truth, psychiatrists would examine him to determine whether he was competent to stand trial, and also whether he had been sane or insane at the time of the murders. If doctors determined he was competent to stand trial but that he had been insane at the time of the murders, he would confess to the crimes, but enter a plea of not guilty by reason of insanity. If, however, psychiatrists concluded that DeSalvo had been sane at the time of the murders, he would not confess. Thus everything would stop because it would mean almost certain conviction. And if he did not confess, there would be no trial, because there would be no evidence on which to indict him. If that happened, DeSalvo could be tried only for the sexual assault crimes he had committed in late 1964.

Bottomly began his questioning of DeSalvo. The goal was to be certain that he was the Strangler. At the first session, Bottomly said, "Albert, I don't think you did all these things. I don't believe it. But I'm here to listen—let's talk about them." Over the next few months, Bottomly asked hundreds of questions, probing for details that could be verified. The details piled up. Bottomly slowly built a wall of facts so strong that it seemed there could be no reasonable doubt that DeSalvo was the Boston Strangler.

Still, DeSalvo refused to talk about two victims. Finally, on September 29, Bottomly asked him some specific questions about the murders of eighty-five-year-old Mary Mullen, one of the victims the police initially had not attributed to the Strangler, and twenty-three-year-old Beverly Samans.

Those questions got DeSalvo talking about Mullen. He described walking up the stairs to her second-floor apartment. He told her he had come to do repair work. She invited him into the apartment. He sat in an armchair, she in a rocker. He paused. "She looked like my grandmother, my mother's mother," he said. "She cared for me." When Mullen stood up from the rocker, he went on, "my arm went around her neck and she went straight down. I didn't want her to fall on the floor." She had died of a heart attack. He placed her on the couch and left the apartment. "I didn't meant to hurt nobody," he said over and over. Now he spoke between gasps. "My grandmother. These things did happen. Why?"

After a silence, Bottomly asked DeSalvo to talk about Samans. DeSalvo began. He had been in Samans's apartment building before, pretending to be a modeling talent scout. When he knocked on her door about eight in the morning, she opened it. He said Samans seemed to be reading his lips, and Bottomly knew that Samans was hearing impaired. When Bottomly asked if there was any unusual furniture in the apartment, DeSalvo correctly said there was a piano and drew, again correctly, a picture of an upright.

DeSalvo continued his story. Once inside her apartment, he pulled a knife and told Samans that he wanted to fondle her, but he promised that he would not force her to have intercourse. He tied her hands behind her and gagged her and fondled her. Although he had gagged her, Samans "wouldn't shut up," and DeSalvo told her he was going to rape her. "Don't do it! Don't do that to me!" Samans yelled; "You lied! Don't do it!" DeSalvo picked up the knife he had laid on a table and stabbed her. "Once I did it once, I couldn't stop," DeSalvo said; then he whispered, "She reminded me of Irmgard."

DeSalvo's confession was completed on September 29, 1965. Bottomly and Bailey were convinced that DeSalvo was the Boston Strangler. After the final interrogation session, Bottomly's tapes were transcribed and analyzed. Detectives Andrew Tuney and Phil DiNatale carefully charted DeSalvo's answers, fact-checking each statement against the records of the murders and trying to determine whether he might have gleaned the information from newspaper accounts or from an insider. DeSalvo's scorecard was impressive. He accurately recalled dozens of details from the murder scenes that would be known only to someone who had been there.

Now the question was what to do with DeSalvo's confession. Bailey wanted to put together a deal that would prevent DeSalvo from being executed and guarantee that he would receive psychiatric treatment.

CHAPTER FIVE

DeSalvo on Trial

O n June 30, 1966, nine months after Albert DeSalvo confessed to the murders of thirteen women, a hearing was held to determine if he was competent to stand trial on eight indictments charging assault and battery with a dangerous weapon, commission of unnatural acts, breaking and entering, larceny, and armed robbery. There were several causes for the delay. For one thing, F. Lee Bailey was extraordinarily busy during the winter of 1965–66. He successfully had argued the Sam Sheppard case before the U.S. Supreme Court and also had convinced the Massachusetts Supreme Judicial Court to reverse George Nassar's death sentence. For another thing, Bailey and Attorney General Edward Brooke, according to Bailey, had tacitly agreed to drag their feet on the Strangler case so that Brooke could launch a campaign for United States Senate. Finally, and most important, Bailey, Brooke, Strangler Bureau chief Bottomly, and a string of attorneys and psychiatrists worked to establish a procedure for trying DeSalvo and to orchestrate an outcome that would be mutually acceptable to the state and to the defense.

Normally, the criminal justice system is adversarial, but Bailey sought the state's cooperation. His goals were: to convince the police that DeSalvo was the Strangler; to convince the court that although his confession was inadmissible, its contents could be used as evidence to prove that he was legally insane and, therefore, he could not be held criminally liable for the several counts of sexual assault for which he was tried; to get the very best psychiatric care for his client; and to avoid the death penalty. The state, for its part, would be assured the Strangler would be off the streets indefinitely.

It was a risky strategy. According to Massachusetts law a jury determined whether to accept a defendant's plea of not guilty by reason of insanity. If a jury found a defendant legally sane—he or she was able to distinguish between right and wrong and did not act as a result of an irresistible impulse—it could recommend that a defendant found guilty of murder be sentenced to death or to life imprisonment. (Although Massachusetts had not executed a convicted murderer since 1947, it seemed highly likely that if a suspect were convicted, a jury would recommend the death penalty for the Strangler. The death penalty remained on the books until 1980.)

At the close of one discussion with Brooke and Bottomly, Bailey explained his offer as follows: "I've helped him disclose that he's committed multiple murders, and it's a certainty he'll never be released. Show me some way to avoid the risk of execution—I'll run the risk of conviction, but not execution—and you can have anything you want." Brooke acknowledged that ordinarily Bailey's plea bargain would be acceptable, but the question of how to proceed against the Strangler was hardly ordinary. The challenge was how to create a win–win outcome rather than the usual win–lose.

Bailey and Bottomly talked about several possible solutions:

Present DeSalvo's confession to the stranglings to a grand jury, expecting that the jury would acknowledge it to be true but not bring an indictment because the confession would be inadmissible at a jury trial. The problem with this proposal was that a grand jury was supposed to make its decision on the basis of evidence, and not whether the evidence it heard would be admissible at trial.

Present DeSalvo's confession to a grand jury that would return a murder indictment but expect that the trial judge would rule the confession inadmissible. Bailey and Bottomly rejected this possibility, realizing that a judge would not be likely to go along with such an unethical deal worked out between a prosecutor and a defense attorney. Besides, under Massachusetts criminal procedure a jury could override a judge's ruling to exclude a confession as inadmissible.

Present unanimous expert medical testimony of DeSalvo's insanity to a trial jury, which would lead the jury to find DeSalvo not guilty by reason of insanity. But a jury could disregard the evidence and find DeSalvo sane when he murdered and recommend that he be executed for the murders he confessed to committing.

These three plans, all admittedly flawed, were shoved aside, however, when Bottomly abruptly resigned from the Strangler Bureau, as well as Brooke's Senate campaign and the attorney general's office, on April 8, 1966. He had had a major disagreement with Brooke, allegedly about a matter unrelated to the Strangler case. With Bottomly gone, Bailey and Brooke met to hammer out a new plan of action. At the meeting, Brooke said the case against DeSalvo could go ahead as soon as detectives took DeSalvo's formal confession. Bailey objected, insisting that months earlier Bottomly and Brooke had agreed to share with the defense the reports from the state psychiatrists who had examined DeSalvo. Brooke said he did not recall such a deal. Bailey then stated he would not allow DeSalvo to confess unless he had assurance that DeSalvo's confession would not lead to his execution. Finally, Brooke and Bailey agreed that DeSalvo would be tried for sexual assault.

The sexual assault charges pending against DeSalvo had nothing to do with the stranglings, but Bailey reasoned that the trial would allow him to question the state's psychiatrists about DeSalvo's sanity. If they testified that DeSalvo was not legally sane, Bailey would allow his client to confess to the murders. On the other hand, if the psychiatrists stated that DeSalvo was sane at the time of the murders, Bailey would ask if they were familiar with DeSalvo's complete mental history: "Does your opinion take into account the fact that he killed thirteen women?" Bailey also planned to put Bottomly on the stand to testify as to what DeSalvo had told him during their long, revealing sessions.

A hearing to determine if DeSalvo was competent to stand trial on the sexual assault charges began on June 30 at the Middlesex County courthouse in Cambridge, with Judge Horace J. Cahill presiding. Inside the second-floor courtroom sat spectators, police officers, one-time Strangler Bureau participants, including Bottomly, and a row of expert witnesses waiting to testify. His dark hair neatly parted and combed to the right side, DeSalvo sat impassively in the prisoner's dock, a small wooden structure about four feet tall and four feet square, open at the top, situated about twelve feet from the tables occupied by his defense counsel and the prosecution team.

Bailey called three psychiatrists, beginning with Dr. Robert Mezer, a private practitioner who had examined DeSalvo at Bridgewater. Mezer said that DeSalvo suffered from "chronic undifferentiated schizophrenia" and required commitment, but he was competent to stand trial. The next psychiatrist, Dr. Samuel Tartakoff, characterized DeSalvo as a "sociopath with dangerous tendencies," but agreed that DeSalvo could help counsel with the preparation of his defense.

Assistant District Attorney Donald L. Conn, a Boston University classmate of Bailey's and the star criminal prosecutor of the Middlesex County district attorney's office, called Dr. Ames Robey to the stand. Robey originally had diagnosed DeSalvo as a borderline psychotic and told the court in 1965 that he was not competent to stand trial. He also did not believe DeSalvo was the Strangler. DeSalvo, said Robey, suffered from "schizophrenic reaction, chronic undifferentiated type with very extensive signs of sexual deviation." He frequently had seen DeSalvo "in a homosexual panic." For that reason, he said, "My opinion is that I cannot—repeat—cannot consider him competent to stand trial." Conn asked Robey how DeSalvo would act under the stress of a trial. He could become "overtly paranoid and indulge in an outburst," Robey answered. Given his psychiatric condition, Conn asked, what might be expected if DeSalvo were to testify? DeSalvo, Robey stated, is a "compulsive confessor," someone who has a "real need, because of his underlying illness, to prove to himself and to others his own importance."

Bailey cross-examined Robey, aggressively pushing him to justify his conclusion as to DeSalvo's competency. DeSalvo might "intellectually know" the charges against him, but he lacked an "emotional awareness" of their seriousness, Robey said. Further, under the stress of cross-examination, DeSalvo would be unable to make sense. Bailey's next question sprung a trap: "To your knowledge, has he been in circumstances of great stress? "No," answered Robey. "He has not?" asked Bailey incredulously. "No," Robey repeated. "Are you aware," Bailey asked, his voice rising nearly to a shout, "that he has been the subject of the most gigantic homicide investigation in the history of the Commonwealth?" Everyone in the courtroom understood that Bailey was referring to the Strangler case.

The defense called Albert DeSalvo. After a few preliminary questions, Bailey went to the heart of the issue. Did DeSalvo understand the charges brought against him? Had he understood the doctors' testimony? Did he understand that his defense to the charges of sexual assault would be not guilty by reason of insanity? To each question, DeSalvo answered yes. Bailey next asked if DeSalvo understood that "there is a risk that you might be convicted." Was he willing to assume that risk? Again, DeSalvo answered yes.

Conn began his cross-examination of DeSalvo by repeating some of the same questions Bailey had asked. But, without changing his tone, Conn's next several questions were directed at the Strangler. "Do you fully understand the implications of your past conduct?" The answer was yes. "Do you understand what can happen to you, sir, as a result of what you have done?" Yes. Did De Salvo make "certain disclosures" to Assistant Attorney General John Bottomly? Yes.

Conn next asked DeSalvo to tell the court under what conditions he had agreed to talk to Bottomly. DeSalvo struggled to articulate an answer, but then said, "I was told that under the conditions anything I said would never be held against me." Conn asked, "And what was the information going to be used for? Were you told?" Judge Cahill warned Conn. Then Bailey addressed the court. "Your Honor, the information was to be used for the benefit of the doctors in determining whether or not this man's history was fact or fiction."

Conn asked if DeSalvo knew what his defense would be. DeSalvo answered, "Yes. Not guilty by reason of insanity." "Do you feel you are sick?" the prosecutor asked. "I feel I am in a mental condition," the defendant answered. "How long have you felt ill?" Conn asked. In answer, DeSalvo briefly traced his "mental condition" to his childhood and suggested that his violent adult behavior was somehow linked to his tumultuous upbringing. He added that he now felt he had to do what he thought was right. "What do you mean by right?" Conn asked. "To tell the truth," DeSalvo answered without hesitation. "And, if by telling the truth I have to be punished, so be it. I have got to do what I feel is right, no matter what may happen to me."

Ten days after the hearing, Judge Cahill held DeSalvo competent to stand trial for the sexual assaults, and on July 11, 1966, he entered a plea of not guilty. The court ordered him held without bail at Bridgewater. For the next six months, while he was awaiting trial, DeSalvo tried to make a positive contribution to life at the state hospital. He worked in the kitchen and washed and shaved elderly male inmates. He also reported to authorities every brutal, uncaring act toward patients he observed, a reform campaign that would help launch an effort to reform the hospital.

Commonwealth v. DeSalvo began January 10, 1967. As he had outlined at the competency hearing, Bailey hoped to convince the jury that DeSalvo was not guilty by reason of insanity of the crimes with which he was charged—breaking and entering, assault and battery, armed burglary, and unnatural and lascivious acts. In addition to the testimony of psychiatrists, Bailey also planned to demonstrate the depth of DeSalvo's insanity by introducing evidence that he had strangled thirteen women. Specifically, Bailey sought to get DeSalvo's confession into evidence and have Bottomly and detective DiNatale corroborate it. In this way he would prove DeSalvo was the Strangler without running the risk he could be executed for the murders.

🔑 🔑 🔑

THE RULES GOVERNING the determination of insanity arose from the assumption that a defendant must be capable of exercising free will in order to be held responsible for a criminal act. Anglo-American law holds it morally reprehensible to punish a person who does not know or understand that what he or she did was wrong. Although this principle is accepted without question, there has long been widespread disagreement among both professionals and the public about the test to determine legal responsibility.

Before the birth of modern psychiatry, the law applied what was called the "wild beast" standard. A defendant could win exemption from punishment according to this test only if there was convincing proof that he or she was "totally deprived of his understanding and memory, and doth not know what he is doing, no more than an infant, than a brute or a wild beast." In 1843 an English court chased the wild beast from the courtroom, but opened a centuries-long controversy when it found Scottish woodcutter Daniel McNaughten not guilty by reason of insanity for the murder of Prime Minister Robert Peel's secretary.

The uproar that followed the verdict in *Rex v. McNaughten* led to an extraordinary meeting of all fifteen high-court judges. The judges generally approved of the new test, but they sought to quiet controversy by adding a cognitive test. A defendant could prove insanity if he was not able to distinguish right from wrong.

The year following McNaughten, the Massachusetts Supreme Judicial Court modified the right-from-wrong test. In *Commonwealth v. Rogers* (1844), the court acknowledged that Abner Rogers knew it was wrong to murder Charlestown State Prison warden Charles Lincoln, but that he was driven by an "irresistible impulse." Defense attorney George Bemis begged the jury to put aside the "common opinion" that a plea of not guilty by reason of insanity was nothing more than a clever excuse for getting away with murder.

More than a century later the Massachusetts court added the "policeman-at-the-elbow" test in an effort to clarify irresistible impulse. In other words, even if a police officer were standing at the side of a person driven by an irresistible impulse, he or she would be unable to resist committing the crime. In 1962 the American Law Institute (ALI) advocated the adoption of a test stating that in order for a defendant to be held responsible under the cognitive test (knowing right from wrong), he or she "must have substantial capacity to appreciate the wrongfulness of his act," and to be held responsible under the irresistible impulse test he "must have substantial capacity to control his conduct so as to be able to abstain from doing the unlawful act." If DeSalvo was convicted, Bailey intended to appeal to the Supreme Judicial Court for a reversal and a new trial by arguing that the court should use the broader and more flexible ALI test.

🔑 🔑 🔑

BEFORE A JURY WAS IMPANELED, Bailey and Assistant District Attorney Conn met with Judge Cornelius Moynihan to discuss whether Bailey could use the stranglings to prove insanity. Moynihan ruled that the psychiatrists were free to refer to DeSalvo's history and background as

Albert DeSalvo arrives at the Cambridge District Court, January 12, 1967, during his trial for multiple sexual assaults. A jury found DeSalvo guilty, and he was sentenced to life imprisonment. **(Boston Globe)**

a basis for their opinion as to DeSalvo's sanity. "If Mr. DeSalvo has told these psychiatrists something of his activities in the years prior to these offenses which influences their judgment, they will be allowed to relate it. But," the judge added, "only as part of that history and for no other purpose."

Assistant District Attorney Conn called four of the women DeSalvo was charged with sexually assaulting, as well as several police officers who had worked on the cases. Each woman told a similar story. DeSalvo had gained entrance to her apartment by using a strip of stiff plastic to slip the lock on the front door. Once inside, he threatened the woman with a knife or toy pistol, forced her to strip naked, bound her, fondled her breasts, and performed oral sex. In his opening statement, Bailey acknowledged DeSalvo's guilt, but he argued that DeSalvo was not legally sane when he committed the crimes. As his first expert witness, he called Dr. James Brussel, the New York psychiatrist who had offered a very different profile of the Strangler than the Strangler Bureau psychiatrists, and who had recently examined DeSalvo. Brussel told the court that after administering a series of tests, he had concluded DeSalvo was a schizophrenic who could not distinguish right from wrong. Under Conn's cross-examination, however, the New York doctor frequently lapsed into jargon that seemed to confuse symptoms with diagnosis.

The next day, Bailey led Dr. Robert Mezer, another expert witness, through a detailed psychological portrait of DeSalvo, beginning with his childhood and concluding with the doctor's analysis of why the stranglings began and ended. Mezer speculated that DeSalvo became homicidal in the summer of 1962 because his wife, Irmgard, had rejected him, insisting he had to prove he had reformed before they could resume normal sexual relations. When that occurred, his homicidal urge became weaker. DeSalvo still craved sexual gratification outside marriage, Mezer explained, but now his urge could be fulfilled without murdering the women he assaulted. In brief, in committing the sexual assault crimes, DeSalvo was driven by an irresistible impulse.

Conn asked Mezer if DeSalvo's sexual impulse would have been deterred by the hypothetical "policeman at the elbow." Mezer answered yes. Conn next asked if DeSalvo's break-ins and robberies were driven by an impulse. The prosecutor's question was aimed at highlighting DeSalvo's rational acts—jimmying the lock of an apartment, ordinary theft—in order to undercut the argument that he was not sane when he committed the assaults. In other words, would an insane man have been able to skillfully pry open the lock of an apartment and choose valuable goods to steal? Mezer answered that not all DeSalvo's behavior was irrational or impulsive; even a person driven by an irresistible impulse was capable of conforming most of his or her behavior to normal standards. Conn knew Mezer's answer was accepted by psychiatrists, but the prosecutor assumed that most jurors did not accept selective insanity.

Bailey thought he gained back some ground when, referring to the ALI guidelines for insanity, he asked Mezer if DeSalvo lacked the capacity to conform his conduct to the requirements of the law. According to this test, Mezer answered, all of DeSalvo's criminal acts resulted from his insanity.

On Monday, Ames Robey testified for the prosecution. His professional diagnosis was that although DeSalvo had a "sociopathic personality disorder," he knew the difference between right and wrong and he was not driven by an irresistible impulse. Two other psychiatrists gave similar testimonies. On cross-examination, Bailey failed to get any of the expert witnesses to embrace the more flexible ALI definition of insanity. And although the defense took exception, Judge Moynihan instructed the jury to disregard DeSalvo's claim to the stranglings. "He is not on trial in this court for homicide," Moynihan asserted.

On January 18, 1967, after deliberating less than four hours, the jury found DeSalvo guilty on all counts. Judge Moynihan sentenced him to life imprisonment. Bailey angrily and dramatically told the press, "Massachusetts has burned another witch." He announced that he would appeal the decision—his first major trial loss—to the Massachusetts Supreme Judicial Court.

The Supreme Judicial Court noted the obvious: the experts agreed DeSalvo was mentally ill and dangerous, but they differed as to whether he could or could not control his impulses. One by one the court punctured Bailey's arguments. The defense claimed it was confusing and prejudicial for the trial court to refer to both the Rogers test—right from wrong—and the ALI test—"substantial capacity to appreciate the wrongfulness of his act." Writing for a unanimous court, Justice Whittemore flatly rejected this argument. In fact, he wrote, it was helpful to the defendant to qualify the Rogers language with the more workable language of the ALI test. Whittemore also denied the validity of DeSalvo's argument that he should have been permitted to introduce evidence to show he had committed thirteen murders. Testimony about the defendant's murderous acts "was plainly inadmissible evidence." The defendant should have proved his inability to control himself "in usual ways." Finally, Whittemore saw nothing unusual in the experts' disagreement over whether the defendant was able to control his conduct or not. Psychiatrists differ all the time. Still, the jury was able to sort the expert testimony and conclude that DeSalvo was responsible for his conduct. There is "no better way to determine" the sanity of a criminal defendant "than by leaving to the twelve citizens of the jury the application of a reasonable and understandable rule after a fair trial and under full and fair instructions. That is what happened in this case." The court affirmed

DeSalvo's conviction and in so doing demolished Bailey's attempt to rewrite the rules for determining a defendant's sanity.

Bailey's argument on DeSalvo's behalf had failed miserably. No experienced lawyer was surprised. For more than a century, trials in which a defendant's sanity was at issue were characterized by sharply differing testimony from psychiatrists. For that reason, among others, courts steadfastly had refused to defer to psychiatrists' opinions and, in nine out of ten cases juries rejected a defendant's plea of not guilty by reason of insanity.

Five years had passed since Anna Slesers was found dead in her Boston apartment. Although Bailey had not succeeded in proving formally that DeSalvo was the Boston Strangler, and although the word "strangling" had not been used during DeSalvo's trial for sexual assault, many women in greater Boston believed their long nightmare was over.

CHAPTER SIX

Aftermath

A
lbert DeSalvo served just seven years of his life sentence. Pending the results of his appeal, the court initially remanded him to Bridgewater, a sprawling facility with more than a hundred buildings spread over fifteen hundred acres. Four distinct populations were housed at the complex: approximately six hundred men and women were under lock and key in the state hospital for the criminally insane; another eight hundred to a thousand alcoholics and drug addicts who had either been sentenced by the court or voluntarily committed themselves were segregated in a jumble of crumbling buildings; one hundred fifty severely mentally retarded juveniles were jammed into another ancient structure; and approximately one hundred fifty sexually dangerous patients were held in a treatment center.

"Albert," Bailey said when DeSalvo complained about the conditions at Bridgewater, "this place is a garbage dump." Bailey encouraged his client to report to authorities every instance of abuse he suffered or observed. DeSalvo did file dozens of formal complaints. And with good reason. Bridgewater State Hospital was an appalling place: not only were the physical surroundings in ill repair, but the inmates were treated poorly. A 1967 documentary exposé, *Titicut Follies* by Frederick Wiseman, captures the deliberate, almost casual cruelty with which the guards and doctors treated the inmates. We see a doctor standing on a chair, force-feeding an old man through a tube in his nose; that scene is interspersed with footage of the same old man's cadaver being prepared for burial. In one of the most moving moments of the film, a young man diagnosed with paranoid schizophrenia begs to be sent back to prison, because Bridgewater has brought him only "harm." DeSalvo felt the same way. His oft-expressed desire to be under the best psychiatric care was smashed when the Cambridge jury spurned his plea of not guilty by reason of insanity. And when DeSalvo complained about how badly he and the other Bridgewater patients were treated, guards grabbed him from the ward, stripped off his clothing, and threw him into an isolation cell.

Shortly after midnight, Friday, February 24, 1967, DeSalvo and two other inmates, a burglar and a convicted murderer, escaped from Bridgewater. They climbed down an elevator shaft under construction and used planks to get over a twenty-foot wall. The three men ran across a field to a road leading to the town of Bridgewater. DeSalvo left a note on his bunk addressed to Bridgewater Superintendent Charles Gaughan. He said his escape was intended to dramatize his own situation and the horrible conditions at Bridgewater. He apologized to Gaughan and assured him that he did not intend to harm anyone.

Once they reached the town of Bridgewater, the three men stole a car and drove toward Boston. They got as far as Everett before the car broke down. DeSalvo called his brother Joseph, who lived nearby. Joseph drove them to Chelsea, where, Richard, another of Albert's brothers, provided him with a change of clothing and drove Albert's companions to a subway station in Charlestown. The two men got as far as Waltham, where they drank steadily throughout the day before turning themselves in on Friday night, less than twenty-four hours after their escape. In the meantime, Albert's brothers gave him some money and dropped him off in Lynn at about 8 A.M.

By this time a full-scale manhunt had been launched for the Boston Strangler. Thousands of police poured into the streets, cruised up and down Boston streets, and searched vacant houses where DeSalvo might be hiding. As one newspaper reporter put it, "It was one hell of a story for 36 hours." Radio and television reported hour by hour. Wild rumors circulated. De Salvo had been spotted walking along a Boston street, in an Ohio airport, en route to Canada.

In fact, DeSalvo spent the day riding buses from one end of Lynn to the other and listening to news of the search for the Boston Strangler. He had one close call. Waiting for a bus, a policeman approached him. "Are you DeSalvo?" No, DeSalvo replied, pointing to a nearby apartment building. "I live right upstairs there—check with my wife if you want." The police officer turned and walked away.

Sometime after midnight, DeSalvo slipped into the basement of a triple-decker. He slept restlessly and in the morning found a sailor's uniform that fit him. On the transistor radio he carried, he heard that the *Boston Record American* had offered a $5,000 reward for him, dead or alive. One of Bailey's associates also broadcast a plea for DeSalvo to turn himself in. By Saturday afternoon he was tired, cold, and hungry, and he was ready to do as Bailey asked. He left his cellar hideaway and walked a few hundred feet to a clothing store. Inside, he asked to use the phone. A clerk said, "Sorry, we don't have a pay station here."

"This is an emergency," DeSalvo shot back. "I got to call F. Lee and I don't have any change."

The clerk pointed to the phone on the counter. While DeSalvo made a call to Bailey's office, the clerk, who had recognized DeSalvo from a newspaper picture, walked to the manager's office and telephoned the police. Within minutes, several Lynn police officers, guns in hand, burst into the store, where DeSalvo was having a cup of coffee with the manager.

At the Lynn police station, DeSalvo repeated, more or less, what he had written in his escape note. "I didn't bother nobody and I never will. I didn't mean no harm to nobody." He explained that he had escaped from Bridgewater "to bring back to the attention of the public that a man has a mental illness and hires a lawyer, and no one does anything about it."

In fact, he succeeded. Although DeSalvo's dramatic escape was not the sole driving force, the Massachusetts legislature launched an investigation and eventually appropriated money for new buildings at Bridgewater. When the state dragged its feet, a federal judge stepped in and ordered the state to make good on its promise.

Following his escape, DeSalvo was transferred from Bridgewater to the maximum-security state prison at Walpole, Massachusetts. Immediately nicknamed "Silky" by the other inmates—an allusion to

Albert DeSalvo emerging from the Lynn, Massachusetts, police station following his escape from Bridgewater State Hospital on February 24, 1967. (Bettman/Corbis)

nylon stockings the Strangler used to murder his victims—DeSalvo was assigned to a floor-washing crew, often working within view of visitors to the prison who sometimes pointed him out as the Boston Strangler. In his spare time he took up jewelry making, specializing in women's necklaces known as "Albert DeSalvo's Chokers." In the fall of 1973 DeSalvo was working as an orderly in the prison infirmary. He was one of eight inmates sleeping in the fourteen-room infirmary area, separated by a metal gate from the medical treatment rooms. Inmates were able to come and go to the medical treatment rooms at any time, but a metal gate locked and controlled by a guard separated the two medical areas.

At 8:48 on the morning of November 27, 1973, Albert DeSalvo was found dead in his cell. The door was locked. He had been stabbed with a small knife or surgical instrument six times in the heart and lung as he lay in his bed. The assailant had turned his body facedown and covered it with a blanket to delay its discovery. A search failed to discover the murder weapon. DeSalvo's murder was the twelfth violent death at trouble-plagued Walpole prison in a two-year period.

The night DeSalvo was murdered, the gate was unlocked, allowing any of the twenty or thirty inmates who entered the infirmary access to the room where DeSalvo slept. Norfolk District Attorney George Burke, whose district included Walpole prison, noted that DeSalvo had had "several beefs" with another inmate in recent weeks. Burke implied that the problems between the two men stemmed from drug dealing. He had once during the previous year threatened to send DeSalvo back to Bridgewater if he didn't stop selling drugs, and that threat seemed to have worked. But, Burke added, it was possible that DeSalvo intended to move back into the business and was murdered by a competitor. Though Burke twice brought charges against three inmates for the murder of DeSalvo, the two trials ended without a conviction.

DeSalvo's death once again raised questions about his claim to be the Boston Strangler. A number of people believed he was not. Some thought that he was a braggart, or that he had murdered the five old women—but that copycats, or boyfriends, or a mental patient known to Dr. Robey, or convicted murderer George Nassar had murdered the younger women. Some even have suggested that attorney F. Lee Bailey and DeSalvo cooked up a confession to reap the financial rewards from a book and movie deal. Ed Brooke, it was said, accepted the bargain offered by Bailey, because putting DeSalvo in prison promised an end to the Strangler's reign of terror and ensured Brooke's election to the U.S. Senate.

Some police officers and detectives who played a peripheral role in the Strangler investigation bolster one or all of these theories by portraying DeSalvo as too soft, too much the lover, too gentle to murder. A Cambridge homicide detective later said DeSalvo did not have "the brutality to strangle women." Boston police officer Jim Mellon and Dr. Robey named anyone but DeSalvo. Recently, Casey Sherman, a Boston television producer, raised some interesting—but not entirely convincing—counter-arguments about DeSalvo's claim to be the person who murdered thirteen women. Specifically, Sherman argues that DeSalvo's confession to the murder of nineteen-year-old Mary Sullivan, allegedly the last of the Strangler's victims, does not fit the facts as stated in her autopsy report. Sherman believes a boyfriend of one of Sullivan's roommates was the killer.

This much is clear. For eighteen months while the New Boston was being built, vulnerable, single women were murdered by a man whose psychotic need to dominate and punish women was thought to be in conflict with gentleness toward and admiration for women. It also says something significant about the culture of the New Boston that popular anxiety and professional misunderstanding about homosexuals was so profound that the link between homosexuality and violence against women was an unquestioned, unwavering presumption. The death penalty was another significant issue brought to public consciousness by the Strangler. Governor Endicott "Chubb" Peabody was tossed out of office in 1965 for saying that his opposition to the death penalty was so strong he would not sign a death warrant were the Strangler caught and convicted. Two years after DeSalvo's death, however, the Massachusetts Supreme Judicial Court found the mandatory death penalty for rape-murder unconstitutional and in 1980 and 1984 ruled that the death penalty for murder was unconstitutional. Finally, it must be recognized that despite scientific gains and increasing sophistication, popular understanding of insanity and our commitment to caring for those men and women judged to be mentally ill is not much different than it was forty years ago.

Because DeSalvo did not come to trial for murder, it cannot be said with absolute certainty that he was the Boston Strangler. Still, strong evidence points to DeSalvo. Before he contacted Bailey, DeSalvo privately and confidentially told a prison psychiatrist he had destroyed thirteen women. On the eve of his trial for sexual assault, DeSalvo "willingly" confessed to Dr. Robert Mezer that he was the Strangler. He described with reasonable accuracy and in minute detail the women he strangled to death, as well as their apartments and their belongings. He confessed in detail to Bailey and Bottomly and begged for their help. Donovan and Sherry, the two homicide detectives closest to the investigation, never wavered in their conclusion that DeSalvo was the man who had murdered thirteen women. Captain James M. McDonald, head of the Boston Police Criminal Investigation Division in 1973, said, "Based on information supplied to the attorney general's office, if [DeSalvo] wasn't [the Strangler] he must have been looking over the strangler's shoulder." Psychotic and unstable as he was, DeSalvo never retracted his claim to be the Boston Strangler. He protested that he was misunderstood, not that he was innocent.

The shadowy, frightening figure of the Boston Strangler receded into the dark history of sexual vengeance. But the memory of a mad man randomly murdering women still reverberates.

FOR FURTHER READING

Robert J. Allison, *Boston: A Short History* (Beverly, Mass., Commonwealth Editions, 2004)

F. Lee Bailey, *The Defense Never Rests* (New York: New American Library, 1971)

Harold K. Banks, *The Strangler* (New York: Avon, 1967)

James A. Brussel, *Casebook of a Crime Psychologist* (New York: Grove Press, 1968)

Gerold Frank, *The Boston Strangler* (New York: New American Library, 1966)

Susan Kelly, "The Untold Story Behind the Boston Strangler," *Boston Magazine*, April 1992

Lawrence M. Friedman, *Crime and Punishment in American History* (New York: Basic Books, 1993)

Roger Lane, *Murder in America, A History* (Columbus: The Ohio State University Press, 1997)

Thomas H. O'Connor, *Boston A to Z* (London: Harvard University Press, 2000)

Casey Sherman, *A Rose for Mary: The Hunt for the Real Boston Strangler* (Boston: Northeastern University Press, 2003)

INDEX

Note: Page references given in *italics* refer to illustrations or their captions.